# Howling at the Sky
# Draconian Architecture
# and the
# Sabian Keys

Roger Williamson

This second edition published 2013
ISBN-13: 978-1440434143

First published in 2002 by

Magus Meta Media

a division of Magus Books, Ltd.

Minneapolis, MN 55414

Copyright © 2002 Roger Williamson


Also by Roger Williamson
The Sun at Night
Lucifer Diaries
Black Book of the Jackal
Tarot of the Morning Star
Calling Up the Spirits
Labyrinth Tales of a Rite of Passage

Recordings
On the Arrival of the Machine and its Mode of Operation


Cover illustration

Sun at Night an original oil painting by Roger Williamson

**Contents**

Part I
The Masque and the Masked 1
Welcome to the Adventure Zone 9
It's Full of Stars 13
QBL 23
Ghosts in the Machine 35
The Shadow Star 53
Summary 65

Part II
Interlude 71
On the Arrival of the Machine and Its Mode of Operation 73
A Brief Explanation of the Machine: Its QBL and Geometric Correspondences 79

Part III
Entering the Adventure Zone 83
Draconian Architecture 89
The Stars Beyond 97
Soul Catcher 105
Angels With Burning Wings Have Knowledge of Fire: The Rite of Set 109
The Howling 119

Part IV
Machines 127
Banishing Machines 129
Invoking Machines 135
Overture Machine 139

Tables 147
Diagrams 151
Bibliography 165
Notes

# Howling at the Sky
# Draconian Architecture
# and the
# Sabian Keys

Roger Williamson

## The Masque and the Masked

"I'm sorry, but I disagree. There is no necessity for mystery beyond entertainment. There is no reality to fantasy; it is purely a vehicle used by weak individuals to escape from the pressures of the world. Granted, we all use it on occasion; but no clear-minded person would ever give it credit by suggesting that it had any power. Next, you'll be telling me that fairies, ghosts and sightings of UFOs should be taken seriously. But why stop there? Let's suggest that I can change the way I think and the way I behave by using magical flimflam techniques outlined by Eliphas Levi, Freemasons and other mountebanks. Unless I fall prey to insanity, I am not going to be meeting denizens of the astral plane or aliens from other worlds. I am what I think; this is what I am. The world is what I touch, see, taste and smell, nothing more."
"In that case, let me present you with a token of your achievement."
With that, before I had time to object, he confidently gripped my left arm with his left hand and with his right, and deftly twisted a red and black beaded bracelet around my wrist.
He leaned back, admiring his work like an artist reviewing a newly finished canvas. Then quite suddenly, with the focused gaze of a predator's stare, his eyes locked with mine. I felt as if I was in the fatal comatose state of a victim.
I do not recall what broke this spell. Maybe it was a sound from outside in the street; or, maybe it was just the fact that once he had proved his dominance over me there was no need to pursue it.
Relieved, I took the time to fiddle with the beads. While turning them around my wrist, my only thought was that I would take them off once I was away from this individual.

# Roger Williamson

"Thank you, you're very kind."

"We will see," he replied.

We sat in silence. I contemplated the fact that I felt horribly intimidated by the presence of this strong-willed individual. Taking me by surprise he inquired, "Perhaps you would allow me the opportunity to demonstrate my point on the power of fantasy?"

He did not wait for my response but abruptly stood and walked towards a heavy wooden door on the far side of the room. He slowly turned toward me and said, "Well, are you ready?"

I shrugged, and commenced to follow him. My assent was obviously a mere formality.

After pressing down on a brass handle, he pushed open the door and led me into a large room that was dimly illuminated by numerous candles that appeared to be arranged in geometric patterns. Burning tapers revealed depictions of archaic mythological scenes on the shadowed walls. The flickering light, captured in the heavy swirling incense smoke, danced to suddenly audible droning music, while activating these illustrations into animated holographic images. The impressions created by the light and smoke were so strong, it seemed as if the figures were actually stepping out from the very walls that held their images. As if that was not enough, even my host began to take on the elastic qualities of the illustration's animation. His face and torso seemed to bend and meld with the rhythm of the ambient atmosphere. He moved like a snake shedding its skin. I felt that at any moment he would mutate into some member of the reptile or insect kingdom.

To distract myself from these growing, disturbing impressions, I tried to discern where the music was coming from, but this offered little relief as it was like an atmosphere. Without center or direction, the very air itself permeated the entire space like a

# Howling at the Sky

living entity. Further attempting to draw myself into rationality, I directed my attention to the floor. Taking up the whole center area of the room was a large yellow circle. Drawn upon this were crudely drawn lavender symbols which could have been letters of an archaic language, or equally, the random daubings of a disturbed mind. At the far end of the room, also painted on the floor, was a triangle, its single point away from me, colored black. It had white letters on it that were similar characters to those painted on the circle. The striking thing about the triangle was that above it rose a six foot tall tripod with its three legs perched on the pointed corners.

"Please, sit in the center of the triangle under the tripod," he directed, while pointing towards it.

I thought about asking some questions that might work towards alleviating my fears; however, thinking this, my hallucinations subsided as quickly as they had arrived. I took a deep breath, walked over to the triangle and squeezed myself between the legs of the tripod, all the while coughing from the intensity of the incense.

I don't know how long I sat in the triangle but it seemed like only a few minutes. I was therefore very surprised when he opened the door through which we had entered and asked me to follow him. Although I sensed having been in the room for only a few minutes with nothing visibly happening, I had the eerie sensation that something had occurred of which I was not fully cognizant. The bracelet had been getting heavier and more burdensome ever since the stranger had first put it on my wrist; so much so, that I had to take it off today. The weight came not so much from its physical presence around my wrist as from the effect it was having upon my life and the direction my life has been going ever since putting it on. In the ensuing period since having it wound around my wrist, I have been confronted by one crisis after another. I realized that I had unconsciously allowed this stranger to impress his will and his assumptions on my being without my permission. This act had the effect of cracking open my universe and populating it with legions of alien intelligence. I realized that my statement to this stranger had been the words of a fool. Like the Fool in the tarot, I fell into the abyss and entered the real world, the world beyond the limits of my senses.

Therefore, this morning, after having had a terrible night of anxiety, I ate my pride and took the bracelet off. I could feel an immediate relief of tension. The gesture made me admit to myself that my brash statement was derived from the logic of an ignorant man.

I decided to venture out and headed towards the Bell and Cannon, an overpriced tourist pub on Museum Street. It retains its turn of the century charming decor but not its turn of the century prices, menu, or clientele.

The bar was very crowded when I arrived. However, with only a little effort I managed to find myself a table at the far end. I had only been seated a few minutes when a young woman came over and asked if she might share my table. It was odd because I had the distinct impression that I had seen her seated across the bar only a few minutes previously.

She was very tall, and in the crowded environment of the bar, as she tried to maneuver to sit, she let her left leg rub against mine. She revealed a few inches of thigh as she crossed her legs in what I felt was a rather wanton fashion. Although the bar was crowded, I couldn't help but feel there was a deliberate motive on her part to insure that I was made aware of her presence.

In contradiction to her suggestive movement, I observed that she was professionally dressed, wearing a neat gray suit. She spoke with a slight London accent that seemed to conceal some other foreign tongue. Maybe I got this impression because of her olive

# Howling at the Sky

colored skin, leading me to think that she was not local but originated from India or from somewhere in the Middle East. Her hair was jet black. I was sure that it was long, but she had it neatly tied back in a professional manner, making her face appear boyish and page-like.

She immediately initiated some polite conversation, which I encouraged with what I considered interesting anecdotes.

I noted that she possessed a worldly quality of confidence. But, in contradiction to this, there lurked a certain vulnerability. I imagined she had followed the dictates of society, only to receive nothing. Maybe it had taken a while, but judging by my increasing attraction to her, she defiantly knew the male drive and how to harness it: you have to be alluring enough to attract attention but you mustn't give too much away. There has to always be that hidden quality, the ability to draw your victim on into that forest of the mysterious. Is it greed in we men that drives us to always aspire to that which we can't possess; a quality that has the consequence of revealing the world to our species; a constant hunger to devour the unknown and make it known because of our fear of what is unknown? Being alive is a desire to experience the unknown and be challenged. How many in our society have this quality? She understood this now, I felt. Although men would never admit it and would moan about a lack of revelation, we in truth are always looking for more; and so, she has decided to leave them wanting. I suddenly recalled my conversation with the stranger on the mysterious and realized now how mistaken was my argument.

We continued our polite conversation for several minutes. She then abruptly rose, said goodbye, thanked me for letting her share the table, and left.

I looked down to pick up my lighter and noticed there was piece of paper at my elbow. I presumed she must have pushed it across the table when I wasn't looking. I picked it up assuming she had left me her phone number; but my indifferent gaze was startled out of inertia by a strange and garish-looking illustration. It was the depiction of a crudely drawn goat's head. I anxiously looked around to see if she was still in the bar but she was gone. I nervously returned my attention to the coarse illustration. Although crude, it had an alluring, hypnotic, mysterious quality. Once again I was reminded of my experience with the stranger. I turned it over and was disappointed to find that it was blank. I put it in my pocket sensing that I had not seen the last of this woman.

I came out onto the street after another pint, conscious of a sense of lost opportunity. Making my way back to New Oxford Street, I took the tube and returned home.

Since meeting this young woman, I have become haunted by her image and this image is dynamically affecting my outer world. Musically, all I can now play is the same short string of notes in the same sequence and rhythm. It is as though I am trying to perfect their chain for some move into another chain, as a gate leads to another sequence of possibility. Again and again, day after day, week after week it's the same droning pace and same repetition of tones. I feel I am a dispossessed man seeking a way back to what I have lost and in the pattern of keys and notes, the blacks and whites, is the cipher that leads to the path of return. It is an overgrown tangled path that I must follow leading back into the past and the ocean of the subconscious from where I came: the land of the blessed, the secret domain.

Today I saw the man who gave me the bracelet walking hand in hand through Lammas Park with the young woman. I don't think they saw me.

Now shadows crawl along the walls as I begin to recall that something half remembered, scenes as from a dream, occurred

# Howling at the Sky

while I sat within the triangle.  Creeping up behind me, these shadows coat me in their umbra and steal my consciousness, holding it hostage in the dream world.

When a tumbler has been used as a vessel for alcohol, a residue of the substance remains.  I felt I had been used as a vessel, and like the tumbler, I was contaminated by the residue of whatever had been poured into me.

# Roger Williamson

# Howling at the Sky

## Welcome to the Adventure Zone

Magical ability is not given or passed on. It is earned through hard work.

Initiation is not given or passed on. It is earned through an individual's ability to confront and overcome crisis when presented with it. The degree of initiation received is proportionate to an individual's ability to deal with the crisis presented.

Magic is not a religion. Magic is the practice of developing individuality and self-empowerment in order to become more than what we presently are.

These concepts provide the fabric of the present work.

Western ceremonial magic, as practiced today, has its roots in the civilization that flourished in the Nile valley many thousands of years ago, the area known today as the country of Egypt. Through the centuries, the topographic area of Egypt has been perceived as the cradle of magical practice. Even the word alchemy[i] is said by some authorities to originate from this region; it being derived from the word *Khem* meaning "Black Land," the ancient name for Egypt. It was given the title "Black Land" because of the fertile black silt brought down by the Nile at the time of its inundation[ii].

The fundamentals of this magical practice are related to the forces of nature operating in the environment of the Nile valley during the course of a year. In the following work I aim to demonstrate how the dynamics of ceremonial magic practiced today are directly related to the cycles of nature experienced in the Nile valley. They are directly cognate to the action of natural phenomena experienced in this area. These aspects include the star of the pole, the constellation of the Great Bear, the star

# Roger Williamson

Sirius, the inundation of the river Nile, the black silt deposited by the inundation, vegetation, the desert, the moon, the sun and wholeness that is the cycle of the year.

By using natural phenomena as symbolic representations of inner processes, we can re-integrate ourselves back into the fabric of the universe from which we have exiled ourselves. Once integrated, we will again be able to understand the music of the spheres and to comprehend the language of their transmissions. Using geometric functions that are the basis of natural growth, we open ourselves up to original states of consciousness and new life situations. This will ultimately lead to a re-evaluation of our life circumstances.

With all forms of magical practice, it is important that they become part of our everyday lives; otherwise, the practice is useless and we would be better off finding an alternative form of recreation. Magic is about changing and experiencing life, not escaping change or life. Magic offers the reward of the unlimited territory that is the Adventure Zone.

The following work is the culmination of many years of experience using the techniques of ceremonial magic as developed by the Order of the Golden Dawn. Most forms of practical magic and witchcraft practiced and written about today owe many of their techniques to this organization; however, few acknowledge the debt they owe this body.

One of the principal points of this order that is often overlooked is that it was not a religion. It was and is a system of attainment that offers individuals a technique to awaken them to their full potential. For the practitioners of this system there are no messiahs or human personalities to be worshipped. What are traditionally spoken of as Gods are seen by the magical tradition as different forms of energy that are manifest in the functions of geometry, colors, musical scales and harmonics.

# Howling at the Sky

Let us now trace the origins of belief and the practice of magical procedure that we may be empowered to spiral into the unknown future with positive results.

# Roger Williamson

## It's Full of Stars

The last words of David Bowman.
*2001: A Space Odyssey*, a novel by Arthur C. Clarke[iii]


*"The more powerful souls perceive truth through themselves, and are of a more inventive nature. Such souls are saved through their own strength."*

Chaldean Oracle


We are immersed in a sea of invisible worlds that go undetected by our senses. The limited range of our everyday faculties gives only an infinitesimal vision of the energies that cohabit the universe with us. Gods, angels, ghosts, phantoms and alien intelligences are incessantly issuing from the invisible void of the infinitely large and the infinitely small to converse with us. In dreams and emotions we are spoken to by these energies but seldom do we give ourselves the time to translate these messages from the void. But in quiet moments and during sleep, these worlds attempt to make contact to re-integrate us back into the fabric of the universe where all is interconnected. Our deeper selves, now also invisible to most of us, struggle to respond and react to the transmitted messages of the void.

In response to this frustration, our bodies and minds revolt in anger, sickness, mental instability and other myriad forms of physical and psychiatric complaints. Daily, we now give ourselves to the messages of man instead of to the forces of our inner-selves. We have sacrificed our individuality and sense of self for the reward of comfort and a false world of safety. Our society promises a condition that does not exist. In giving ourselves to this falsehood, we have relinquished our will and severed ourselves from the current of life that is adventure. As a species and as individuals, we are losing our ability to adapt to the new and original situations that life offers us as tests to our continued existence as vehicles of its expression. We now tend to view these new life situations as hostile instead of challenging.

This attitude is not a modern phenomenon but has been developing since the emergence of so-called "civilized man." To our ancestors, communication with these invisible realms was a source for gathering knowledge. This can still be witnessed today by observing nomadic tribes. Those we like to call "primitive" people, are able to find the location of game and water for their needs without any apparent logical method. They can also heal the sick and can predict the unfolding of future events. These people are a closer part of the great cycle of existence. They know its laws and they know these laws are the laws of nature. This is not to say that our technological achievements do not have a place in our lives. On the contrary, they do. Unfortunately, these external achievements, instead of working with our inner world, have usurped it and cut it off. Observation of humanity's evolution shows a drive toward creating more comfortable and safe surroundings for itself at the expense of individuality and selfhood. We need to learn that the inability of an individual or species to confront

# Howling at the Sky

and adapt to challenging situations will eventually lead to its demise.

Humanity's obsession with safety has even been introduced into our myths. The forces of life, symbolized by the figures in myth, are now personified as good and bad instead of whole or challenging qualities. Such images as Cain and Set have become something to be abhorred instead of being seen as dynamic powers of change and transforming principle. I have endeavored in the relevant passages of this book to demonstrate, using the language of the QBL[iv], that these energies are the driving force of life and to deny them reduces our potential to live. Through their intervention we achieve wholeness, seen as good, but by the same token they change wholeness by metamorphosis into another form. This action is generally seen as bad because it is the loss of what we presently possess.

The present situation, for the vast majority of humanity, is that we have bought into a make-believe world of safety with the currency of our individual will. We allow ourselves to be kept within certain limits and to sacrifice our dreams. It is easy therefore to understand the emergence of conspiracy theories that suggest there are elite groups attempting to control the vast multitude of humanity by the promise of this illusion of safety. However, I believe these restrictions are brought on more by a part of the human condition than by a deliberate conspiracy. Therefore, it should be the work of each of us to develop and overcome the limitations imposed on us by our own species. The adversity we need to overcome is that of complacency.

Prevention is better than cure, but unfortunately as a species we have not taken the preventative measures required to insure our healthy, continuing contact with the force of life. It is time for us to make a shift in perspective and to realign our attitudes to the gift we have been given, life. We need to experience the adversities life offers as opportunities so that the dormant fire of our limitless possibilities may be reawakened. Look at yourself and say, "What am I doing with the gift I have been given?" Record and then meditate on the excuses you come up with for not being more than you are.

Working with the dynamics of the QBL, we can build the vehicle of self-empowerment, the Merkabah[v]. Our attitude to life's new and original situations is the key. All our endeavors need to be focused on cleansing our attitudes of negativity so that we may better interact with life. Negativity is the quality of wholeness that fears to lose what it has achieved. When presented with a situation that is challenging, consider how you might unlock its puzzle instead of slipping into the despair of having to work. There are many systems now available that offer enlightenment and self-empowerment. Each in its own right is as good as any other. However, if the system you are practicing is not impacting on your everyday life, then it is an entertainment only.

What I have endeavored to provide in this book are thought-inducing practical systems of self-empowerment. It is my hope that they will equip the reader with tools to

# Howling at the Sky

better participate in the current of life. I want to encourage readers not to take situations in life at face value, but to look beyond their apparent meanings and to inquire into what life, expressed by their own inner selves, is trying to tell them. We may wish to deny these truths because they demand action and transformation, but in denying them we can never truly express the gift we have been given.

There are many references in this book to the cards of the tarot. I would recommend the purchase of a deck if you do not already have one. It will help you better understand relevant passages. I would suggest you use one of the Golden Dawn decks as they most accurately illustrate the Major Arcana cards' relationship to the zodiac[vi]. The signs of the zodiac are symbolic representations of the forces of nature operating in the Nile valley at particular times of the year. One might argue, "How can natural phenomena, occurring in Egypt, relate to me when I am not living there?" This is a valid argument until one recognizes that the natural phenomena of this area is used as an analogue for representing processes of synthesis and crisis within us[vii].

As an example, the Lovers card illustrates the state of the Nile valley when the sun is in the sign of Gemini. Gemini is the sign preceding Cancer on the wheel of the zodiac. It is in the sign of Cancer that the star Sirius rises with the Sun to announce the inundation of the Nile, which will return life to the land. Therefore, when the Sun is in Gemini, the land is at its most barren. For the ancient Egyptians, this would have been the last sign of their zodiac. The first sign is Cancer, the place of the rising of a new current, announced by the rising of the star Sirius. If we look at the Lovers card, (see diagram 1-01 which is taken from the tarot deck, Tarot of the Morning Star), we see visible nature depicted as a woman, the goddess Isis, chained to a rock or the stump of a dead tree. Rising from the barren landscape is a great serpent, poised to devour what remains of nature. This serpent has, over the course of the year, consumed all of the life-giving water and reduced the land to desert. All would be lost if it were not for the figure in the top left of the card. Here is the adventurer, with sword raised, poised to slash open the serpent who will release the waters of the inundation, realized in the sign of Cancer and illustrated in the tarot card of the Chariot. The figure of the adventurer is the constellation of Orion, often referred to as the hunter. In one image, this card is allegorizing the climax of the quest, the searching for the source of life. You might want to consider a more occult interpretation which is.

*On first view, it appears the male hero is liberating the maiden from the dragon. However, on closer scrutiny, it can be seen that the maiden holds and leads the dragon by the chain around its neck. The dragon is not her jailor but her pet.*

*The maiden is the symbolic stimulus for overcoming fear for she inflames the hero to action liberating him from what holds him back as represented by the dragon.*

*It is not the maiden who is liberated but the male when his desire for her is strong enough to overcome his*

# Howling at the Sky

*fear.*

In periods of our lives when we become bereft of ideas or emotion, we need to call on our intuitive ability, the energy represented by the Lovers card. The card illustrates the comparison of these barren intervals in our lives with the Nile valley prior to the inundation. Our expectations are restrained and appear to be drained of vitality, placing us in a state of inertia. However, the thrill of new possibilities can be liberated by tapping the current of life, the serpent, and by our passion to live, the adventurer, the constellation of Orion. In experiencing this card in barren periods of our lives, we have at our command the tool for unlocking the infinite prospects open to us. Through intuitive ability, we realize that we can be more than what we presently are.

The card following the Lovers, the Chariot, illustrates the result of unleashing these possibilities and the danger of being swept away by them. The interpretation of the Chariot in a tarot reading is ruthless overcoming of obstacles, recovery and success although this may be only temporary. The degree and duration of success will depend upon the amount of work we have done to prepare ourselves for the new life situations that our enthusiasm for life has created for us. The Strength card, which follows the Chariot, illustrates the need for creative discipline and finesse, the requirements needed to channel the released energies constructively if we are to avoid being devoured by them. This card is the achievement of working the machines in *The Black Book of the Jackal.* These machines are provided in Part IV of the present work. They build the circuits necessary for successful assimilation of the energies of the life current.

The card of the Hermit shows the disposition of the successful vehicle of life's possibilities. He/she draws energy from within and does not have a need to egotistically express it outwardly. The life current is contained and prudently expressed through the directions of the inner self rather than by the whims of the outer world.

In the following card, Justice, we see the re-establishment of order from the chaos unleashed by the inundation. Primal energy, released by the inundation, is represented by the wolf, now controlled through correct action, depicted by the figure holding the scale and the sword, the symbols of the astrological sign of Libra. The black and white squares are the floor plan of the future. In the Nile valley, this would be the reallocation of the land as it emerged from the confusion of the inundation. The black and white pillars illustrate the basis of existence as duality, and fairness as the correct application of these energies.

Libra is the astrological sign assigned to this card. It is the seventh sign of the Western zodiac and is ruled by the planet Venus. Seven, on the Tree of Life, is the Sephirah Netzach, meaning "Victory," and to it is assigned the planet Venus. In this card we are observing a state of wholeness achieved through the victory of overcoming adversity. However, this state is not an end but a beginning, illustrated by the card of Justice, number 11 of

# Howling at the Sky

the tarot, the same number as the Sephirah, Daath, on the Tree of Life. Daath is the root of form, yet is itself without form because it is energy and energy is change. In the Justice card, we are witnessing that wholeness is a beginning, a beginning that will be manifested in the following card, Death, and the astrological sign of Scorpio.

At this point we move into Part III of the present work.

I have included these rudimentary remarks on selected tarot cards to illustrate how our inner selves speak in the language of the universe. We, and the universe of which we are a part, are of one mind.

# Roger Williamson

# QBL

*The Illusion of the Magus is Balance.*

There is a message continually being transmitted from the void. Like radio waves, it invisibly permeates all things.

By using a system known as the QBL, we can construct a mechanism to receive and translate this message. The better the QBL is understood, the better the clarity and accuracy of the message received.

The message being transmitted gives details on how to construct a vehicle to transcend time and space. When used, it offers us the ability to travel between differing realms of reality, the vacuum of inter-galactic space, and to communicate with the denizens who inhabit these realities.

The QBL is composed of color, sound and the laws of geometry. The correct understanding of these components and their interrelationships with each other are the substance of the vehicle of attainment called the chariot of Merkabah, the double cube. The Merkabah, Throne Chariot of God, was believed in early Cabalistic literature to offer shamanic experience through levels of heavenly realms as detailed in the vision of Ezekiel. In modern language, the Merkabah is a vehicle used to experience different realms of reality. The objective of experiencing these realms of reality is to expand our consciousness to its full potential that we might live more dynamic and exciting lives.

A shortcut to these realms can be obtained by the use of drugs. However, this method of passage, although offering the experience of the realm, does not necessarily provide an understanding of its language or dynamics or the ability to control the dialogue or experience.

One should refer to the tarot card of the Moon for the

symbolism, dangers and precautions necessary when utilizing the shortcut method[viii].

There are many doors leading from this world into the infinite, and the QBL is just one of many entrances.

For this work the QBL is our guide into unknown territory.

The QBL is a dynamic principle. It is not an object, thing or religion. That is not to say that certain parties have not made it any or all of these things. It is a system of attainment that expands our consciousness by taking us from the world with which we are familiar into the unknown realms that we can, with experience, make our own. The QBL is the action of life and because it is life, it is a testing ground for our worthiness to continue in its adventure.

The language of this unknown territory, as stated previously is, color, sound and geometry. It is paramount that we quest into these realms if we are to understand the basic applications of these energies, in this world, the worlds beyond and the interrelationships between them.
Understanding of these realms is achieved by realigning ourselves to the universe through practicing the exercises detailed in *The Black Book of the Jackal*. These exercises are the gate of direct astral experience where the language of energy is communicated to us. It is here that we are empowered to develop our personal system of reference to confront the challenges of the adventure zone.

The technique is called magic and it must have an impact on our lives. Magic is performed to bring vitality and adventure into our lives by awakening the current of the life force within us. With this awakening will come the awareness that we have the choice to be more than we presently are, that there are multiple possibilities open to us, that we have command over our destinies and that we are accountable for our actions.

# Howling at the Sky

If we do not allow magic to impact on our lives, then our magical practices become an entertainment and an escape from reality.

Magic is the opposite of escaping from life. It is practiced so we may be enticed to fully participate in life's drama. Our strengths and weaknesses must become exposed so that we might work with them to be more suitable agents of life.

I do not intend to give a deep description of the QBL. There are many good titles that already cover this subject.

For the reader who may not be familiar with the subject, I will give a brief synopsis on how the QBL relates to the system of self-empowerment presented in this book.

The QBL is a reference system that can explain the transition of any idea from concept to conclusion. This can be the concept of God as non-being becoming existence, or of an idea becoming a conclusion in three-dimensional reality. It is also an ideal tool for individuals of different doctrines to discuss in a common language the interpretation of their beliefs. The QBL used in this way, as a vehicle of reference, can escape the pitfall of fanaticism, and give people of different belief systems a basis for the exchange of concepts and an understanding of the interrelationship of their philosophies.

For the common image of the QBL, (see diagram 1-02). This illustration is called the Tree of Life. The Tree of Life is composed of ten spheres known individually as Sephirah and twenty-two paths which connect these Sephiroth.

The Sephiroth are actual things or states of being, while the paths are the action of the root powers of geometry which are transforming principles. The Sephiroth are form and the paths are force. These two principles are what make up existence. In alchemy, these principles are represented by the quality of sulfur, the symbol of force and function, and by salt, the principle of fixing or structure. The balanced application of these two principles creates consciousness, the quality of mercury, existence[ix].

The top sphere is called Kether and is purely archetypal. The lowest sphere is Malkuth, the world of the actual, the realization of what was first conceived in Kether.

Each Sephirah has a list of correspondences to enrich the idea represented by it. It is important to note that the Sephiroth are not these correspondences but that there is a relationship between the Sephiroth and the correspondences. See Aleister Crowley's *777* and *Godwin's Cabalistic Encyclopedia* for commonly accepted correspondences. I would suggest however, that it is more rewarding for you, through experience, to develop your own system of correspondences.

The paths are the energies of the Hebrew letters, see ( 1-03), and each letter is associated with a number. Giving the letters numbers however, is somewhat misleading as a number is *something* and the letters, as stated, are transforming principles. The letters are dynamic powers, creative impulses, not things. They are the transition from one Sephirah, state of being, to another Sephirah or state of being. The term ratio is a better way to understand how to access the power of the letters as ratio is a measure of difference. The letters also have a list of correspondences. The most important correspondences are the meaning of the letter, number of the letter, tarot card and color (see tables 1 and 2).

The structure of the Tree of Life is arranged in several ways, operating on several levels of reality.

First, there are the three pillars(see 1-04).

The Pillar of Severity is on the left, comprising the 3rd, 5th, and 8th Sephirah. It is assigned to the element of water.

The Pillar of Mildness is in the middle, comprising the 1st, 6th 9th and 10th Sephirah. It is assigned to the element of air.

# Howling at the Sky

The Pillar of Mercy is on the right, comprising the 2nd, 4th and 7th Sephirah. It is assigned to the element of fire.

Second, there are four worlds to the QBL:

Atziluth: pure deity, archetypal

Briah: creative

Yetzirah: formative

Assiah: the world of nature, human existence and three-dimensional reality

(see diagram 1-05)

These four worlds of the Tree of Life relate to the four tarot suits and the four elements of fire, water, air and earth:

Atziluth: Wands, fire

Briah: Cups, water

Yetzirah: Swords, air

Assiah: Pentacles, earth

Each Sephirah and path is allocated a color for each of the four worlds (see table 2).

    The color scales are used in the construction of magic circles, talismans, amulets, magical weapons and telesmatic images that are pictorial representations of energy derived from the formula of Hebrew names. The scales utilized depend upon the sphere of operation the magician wishes to contact. As an example, to construct a telesmatic image of the name AHIH, אהיה [x]the divine name of Kether, the colors are taken from the Atziluth scale. The head is bright pale yellow, the upper body blood red, the lower body yellowish green, the legs and feet blood red. However, because of the archetypal quality of Atziluth, the image will be seen as swirling, spectral colors rather than as a clear image. As you move down the worlds of the Tree of Life, telesmatic images become clearer and more defined. In Yetzirah, for example, the zoomorphic[xi] images of astrology can be used in their appropriate colors and in Assiah the elemental symbols can be utilized. Refer to table 3 for the hierarchies of the four worlds.

Magic circles are receivers and therefore partake of the Sephiroth. They are constructed to attract a specific energy. In the case of Chesed, the Sephirah of Jupiter, the circle would be blue and the letters orange[xii] when channeling its energy from the Briah scale.

Talismans are symbols of empowerment and as such are representative of energy; therefore they partake of the paths. To be empowered with the energy of Mercury for emotional thinking, such as writing a poem or a work of fiction, one would use the colors of the Briah scale. The background would be light purple and the figures and letters light yellow, the flashing color. For purely academic results you would use the Yetzirah color scale.

Amulets, symbols of protection and refuge, are associated with the known and so have a close affinity with the magic circle. Amulets are generally assigned to the Sephiroth of Assiah, the realm of the everyday world.

The traditional name of God from the Old Testament of the Bible, יהוה, IHVH, permeates all existence and can be allocated to the four worlds of the Tree of Life, the four elements and the court cards of the tarot. This is because the name is representative of the rhythm of life. י is the father, ה the mother, ו is the son and ה is the daughter. The daughter contains the potential of the future, who when activated by the son, becomes the mother, and he becomes the father. However, this incestuous translation of the formula leads nowhere and only perpetuates the continuation of the known order. It is only when the son is attracted outside of the circle to seek a daughter from another circle, or the daughter of one circle attracts the son of another circle, that an explosion of possibility occurs. In the court cards of the tarot, this is demonstrated by the Princess of Wands

# Howling at the Sky

attracting the Prince of Cups, the Princess of Cups attracting the Prince of Swords and the Princess of Swords attracting the Prince of Pentacles (see diagram 1-06).

The Princess of Pentacles hangs in a vacuum at the bottom of the four worlds of the Tree of Life and attracts a whole new system of reference as can be seen in diagram 1-06. The Princess of Pentacles, although the last card of the deck, is the incubating womb of the future and the entrance into untapped potential, the gate of infinite possibility.

Atziluth: י, Fire, Knight

Briah: ה, Water, Queen

Yetzirah: ו, Air, Prince

Assiah: ה, Earth, Princess

The court cards of the tarot also relate to the Sephiroth of the Tree of Life.

Chokmah: Knight

Binah: Queen

Tiphareth: Prince

Malkuth: Princess

From this it can be seen that the tarot interacts well with the Tree of Life.

Each of the four worlds contains a whole Tree of Life and each Sephirah in each of these worlds, contains a Tree of Life. By adding all of these Sephiroth in the four worlds, one discovers that there are four hundred Sephirah, which is the numerical value of ת, the final letter of the Hebrew alphabet. The following are examples of alternative configurations:

- The world of Yetzirah can be divided into seven levels corresponding to the seven Elohim. This world is the body of the Merkabah. (see diagrams 1-07a and 1-07b)

The Elohim אלהימ are the androgynous quality of the One God. It is illustrated by

the word as a feminine noun אלה with a masculine plural ים. Each of the seven
Elohim are assigned to a planet and allocated to the composite figure of the
hexagram. Each point of the hexagram is attributed a planet and the center is
assigned to the Sun. (see diagram 1-08)
- In man, the world of Assaih, the Tree is divided into three, Neschamah, Ruach and Nephesch. (see diagram 1-09)

To Neschamah are allocated the Sephiroth Kether, Chokmah and Binah, corresponding to the highest aspirations of the soul, the intellectual world and the alchemical quality of sulphur.

Chesed, Geburah, Tiphareth, Netzach , Hod and Yesod are allocated to Ruach, the moral world of reasoning powers which determines the nature of good and evil. To the Ruach is allocated the alchemical quality of mercury.

Malkuth is Nephesch, the animal soul and all its desires, material and sensuous, yet containing the Shekhinah, the emanation of God's invisible glory, the flame of life. The alchemical quality of salt is allocated to the Nephesch.

The letters of the Hebrew alphabet, when composed into words, are representative of formulas. This can be compared to musical terms such as the combination of notes creating a chord. In the case of God names, knowing the formula of a name will empower an individual with the energy represented by that God name.

For example, the God name IHVH, יהוה, has a value of 26 if one adds the numerical value of each of the Hebrew letters composing the name. The understanding of this formula, יהוה, gives the magician knowledge to deal with adversity, the attribute of this God name. It is interesting that 26 is also equal to the Sephiroth of the Middle Pillar of the Tree of Life, 1+6+9+10, the pillar of balance. Other correspondences of 26 are, the 26th path of the QBL allocated to the Hebrew letter ע, the path between Tiphareth and Hod, whose tarot attribution is the Devil and the

# Howling at the Sky

Hebrew word כבד, "to honor." This system of deriving an expanded meaning of a word by comparing it with words of the same numerical value is called gematria. The principle of gematria is that words with the same numerical value have an accord, or harmonic resonance, with each other.

When endeavoring to unlock the essence of a name, you can also analyze the tarot cards associated with the letters so you can enhance your understanding. In the case of יהוה we have, Hermit, Emperor, Hierophant, Emperor. The meanings of the Hebrew letters should also be referenced to augment the interpretation. י is hand, ה is window, ו is nail, and the repeated letter ה is again window.

It is for the magician to meditate upon all of these ideas and any other correspondences at his/her disposal. In time, this will assimilate them into a coherent image of the energy and action represented by this God name.

To know the name of a God, meaning to understand its formula, empowers the magician with the power of that God (God being another name for energy). Remember that each of these God names represents a specific action emanating from one energy that is the source of everything, the life-current behind all things. However, it will become apparent through reading the following text that I believe this One God to be dual in action. That the One God is a function and not an item that can be represented by a Sephirah or thing.

If you are experimenting in astral vision, knowing the numbers of the Hebrew alphabet will be very rewarding. You will be able to check the authenticity of personalities met within a vision by referencing their numbers. As an example, when questioning an entity, ask its number. After the vision, you can check to see if this number has a correspondence to the plane you were experiencing. If you find the number has an affinity with the plane then the validity of the experience is that much more correct; if not, then there has been an error somewhere in your working which you will need to research. If you are working with another party this system can be taken to another level. Let one of you be the traveler and your colleague be the scribe. If the scribe knows his numbers, you will be able to converse with astral entities in number by checking their number replies with another corresponding number. This system can be expanded by using the color scales of the Tree of Life and checking their color correspondences from the experiences observed within the vision. In this way there is less chance of deception through your own ego influences.

Initial experience with the system reveals that by playing with numbers and their relationships to each other it is possible for your ego, the Ruach, to come up with practically anything such as adding the numbers, reversing them, multiplying them etc. However, with continuing experimentation you begin to transcend the ego and find that some experiences prove more valid than others. The valid experiences provide positive results and replies to questions asked of entities encountered, and do not offer ambiguity. On these occasions you know you have found the correct key to turn on the engine of the plane in question. You will then be empowered with that plane's energy. Remember the important thing is to experiment and find out for yourself.

The subtitle of this chapter, QBL, is an example of interpreting a name to better understand its meaning.
Q is the Hebrew letter ק meaning the back of the head that represents the sub-conscious; the Tarot attribution is the Moon meaning illusion or imagination.
B is the Hebrew letter ב meaning house; the Tarot attribution is the Magus.

# Howling at the Sky

L is the Hebrew letter ל meaning the ox goad that is guidance; the Tarot attribution is Justice.

In this example, on first examination, it would appear that the Illusion of the Magician is that he/she is in Balance. Another interpretation is that the subconscious of the Magician is the Residence of his Guidance, that it is from the subconscious that he/she seeks the answers to life's challenges. However, it could be explained that the Magician is using his/her imagination to achieve balance, meaning that the magician is traveling the path of ק Qoph. In so doing he/she is moving from the state of Malkuth to a more synthesized and complete state in Netzach. By traveling the path of ק the adventurer is traveling several paths simultaneously, namely, ת Universe, ש Judgment, ר Sun, צ Star, פ Tower and the path ק Moon itself. This is because the path ק connects Sephiroth 10 and 7 directly. See diagram 1-03 of the Tree of Life.

At the beginning of this chapter I stated that the tarot card of the Moon illustrates dangers and precautions necessary for experiencing altered states of reality with the use of drugs.

Now that the fundamentals of the QBL have been outlined I feel it appropriate to describe what was implied by this statement.

The card of the Moon is allocated to the path of ק on the Tree of Life, the path that connects the sephiroth of Netzach and Malkuth[xiii]. The astrological sign attributed to this path is Pisces, the twelfth and final sign of the modern zodiac. In the foreground of the card is a crustacean emerging from a circular stagnant[xiv] pool. The circle represents a revolution, completion and the cycle of a year[xv]. The crustacean[xvi], the transforming principle, is emerging from the past year to travel the path before it that is the circumference of a larger circle as yet not realized as a circle. At the entrance to this path is the jackal god, Anubis[xvii], the guide through the underworld. Howling at the moon, the image which dominates this card, Anubis is alerting us to the dangers of this astrological body's quality, illusion. The illusion of the path is fear and it is fear that we must overcome if we are to become whole[xviii]. Below the Moon are four Hebrew י that add up to forty, the number of the letter מ that has the tarot attribution of the Hanged Man[xix]. The two towers in the center of the card are Geburah and Chesed, the Sephiroth before the Abyss, limits of the rational realm and the conclusion of the world we are about to depart from. They represent the understanding of correct action, which is the function of the Ruach. The back ground color of this card is purple, a color of Daath that represents the paths in total and the veil that conceals the Supernals. As the ninth sign of the Egyptian zodiac, it represents giving birth[xx], which is the death of energy in becoming form. This is the rebirth of the adventurer, the constellation of Orion, who will release the waters of the inundation in the sign of Cancer[xxi].

The word QBL translates in Hebrew as, "to receive," and as a receiver partakes of the symbolism of the cup and grail.

A study of grail mythology reveals that the individual who has become drained of life in the single minded quest for the grail is the one refreshed by the fountain of energy received upon its discovery.

The Grail legends show us that we need to be receptive and open to new ideas, qualities of the grail, if we are to become infinitely energized. This receptive quality is the key to immortality.

# Howling at the Sky

## Ghosts in the Machine

*Female they are not, male they are not.*
Akkadian hymn


*A religion should congratulate itself when its members, having achieved a sense of self, leave its pale. This demonstrates that the religion has achieved its objective, which is to empower its members and not just propagate itself.*


    The term Forces is used throughout instead of the traditional term Gods so the reader does not attribute human or animal gender to these Forces.
The Forces are representative of the forces of nature; they are not human, nor are they superhuman. They are life's functions, aspects of existence that are creation and destruction, leading to synthesis.
    The terms creation and destruction can be misleading until they are understood as being one energy, the current of life. When the life force is observed as creative, we are witnessing its restriction in manifested forms that limit and restrict its flow, so destroying it. What is commonly referred to as destruction is the escape and expression of the life-force from the confinement of a form. However, by escaping, it creates. Construction and destruction are the same single energy divided only by our perspective on how it impacts upon our lives. An act of construction to one individual may be viewed as destructive by another as illustrated by the expression, "One man's sunset is another man's sunrise." Meditation on the Tower card of the tarot will assist in elucidating these concepts.
    We give the Forces forms to rationalize their qualities, but, we need to remember that they are without form because they

are generative powers through which forms appear and change into other forms. They are dynamic functions forming links between heightened states of being, in constant interaction and process, and the actual world of three-dimensional reality. When giving energy form, we kill it.

We, as humans, are temporary expressions of the life-force, vibrations and ripples across the ocean of the infinite, just like anything else which exists. We are no better and no worse. When we are no longer able to change and adapt, life has no further use for us. Life will then depart to find a more adventurous and plastic medium to express itself. We will die to return to the reservoir from which life draws the material for the phases of its manifestations.

Creation, destruction, birth and death are all functions that can be represented in the symbol of the gateway[xxii]. It is through this gate that we step into the unknown future to be devoured by the universe. In nature, we witness this in the dramatization of the eater and the eaten, where the eaten is assimilated into the body of the eater and becomes a part of that larger existence.

Originally, the energies represented by the forces were the elements of nature: fire, water, wind, etc., emphasizing their non-human character. In time, they took animal form, zoomorphic images as tribal totems, and finally, were reduced to human aspects with human frailties and personalities.

You have only to read any of the Greek myths to discover this transformation, where they are reduced to their lowest factor. The energies of life, represented by the Forces, should not be emotionally conditioned as good or bad. They are the raw drive of life pushing outward toward achieving phases of synthesis. We, however, have made these forces of nature symbolize our emotions and then have projected these emotions

# Howling at the Sky

back on to nature with the qualities of good and bad.

What we have intentionally or unintentionally endeavored to do is de-vitalize the forces of nature to create a make-believe universe, a safe place to live. This is in direct opposition to the attitude of the magus who creates a universe in which to be challenged and grow.

Life does not seek preservation. It seeks expression. We, with our human frailty, seek to turn this around. We seek security in preservation. Security, however, comes not from preservation but from learning to ride the current of life, dealing with new and original circumstances. Life is the moment. It is now. Each instant we are alive we are at the threshold of a gateway[xxiii] that opens before us offering original life situations, and behind us are the memories of our past experiences. We should learn from the past in order to impact on the future and be ready to invest what we have achieved to vitalize the unfolding drama of our lives. This act of investment is called sacrifice. It is our readiness to give up our achievements so they may provide us with a vehicle to transport us into the future. A rocket launched into space uses this principle by shedding its boosters to obtain altitude and free itself from gravity. A snake emerges with a new skin that will be a vehicle needing to be shed or sacrificed when it has outlived its usefulness. In farming, the farmer must take part of what he has accumulated and plow it back into the earth to provide the vehicle for what he will reap the following year. He knows he does not own what has been harvested, it is only on loan and must be returned. By watching nature we can learn how to live.

For our ancestors, the forces of nature were neighbors and family, all cohabiting and interacting with one another. All were seen as a part of one great universal energy. As we evolved, it became apparent to certain individuals that the elemental forces of nature directly impacting on their lives had regular periods of action. In observing the night sky these individuals deduced that specific periods of elemental force corresponded to the rising and falling of specific astrological bodies and constellations. These intuitive ancestors then became empowered with the ability to predict future events by synthesizing the movement of the heavens to the actions of elemental energies operating in their environment. With the passing of generations, the actions of elemental forces became transferred to the constellations and planets that announced them. The origin of astrology and religion was born.

Intuition is the ability to assimilate and make cognizant diverse pieces of information into a synthesized pattern. Intuitive ability made certain individuals the magicians of their tribes. Because they understood time, the regular recurrence of events, they appeared to have a command over natural phenomena. The forces of the sky, astrological bodies, spoke to the intuitives and alerted them to the coming arrival of elemental forces. By understanding the cycles of time, which is rhythm, we gain greater command over our destinies. If we know the powers that are coming into play, we are better able to choose how we will react when confronted with them. An understanding of time, the ability to recognize rhythm or cycles, is the basis of magic which is a system of self-empowerment. By interpreting rhythms, we are better equipped to make decisions regarding the course of our lives. In many magical practices, such as voodoo, rhythm is the fabric of the philosophy translated through the medium of drumming. Intoxicated by rhythm, we can be thrown into our subconscious minds, untapped memory banks, and receive from our ancestors memories of primordial cycles of nature.

The greater our understanding of the rhythms of nature of which we are a part, the better able we are to follow our true life course which is expression of the life force. Rock and roll was called the devil's music by established society because of its basis, which was beat. The phenomena of rock and roll is an example of the escape of energy from restriction that threatened the established order. It was an expression of energy releasing itself from the restriction of a Victorian mindset. Intoxication, induced by rhythm, released individuality and individuality is not what established society seeks. Individuality is following your true life's course, unimpeded by your ego, society, religion or other restraints developed by so-called "civilized" society.

To discover our true life course, we need to delve into ourselves and discover what we really are so that we can discern where we should be going. Introspection returns us to our origins and the elemental energies that made us in the crucible of creation. By tapping primal elemental energy, we discover the grail that will refresh our restricted bodies with freedom of individuality and crown us with the knowledge of what we truly are. We discover the grail in the achievement of adjusting ourselves to the current of life. It is to once again walk amongst the forces of elemental energy.

In both the QBL and Ancient Egyptian culture, there are seven primal forces that represent the elemental forces of nature that are assigned to the six directions of space and its center. In the QBL the seven forces are the Elohim that can be represented by the six points of the hexagram and its center. Each point on the hexagram is assigned a planet, and the center is represented by the Sun (see diagram 1-08). If you add the numerical values of each of the planetary paths from, Table 1, you obtain 709, 7+9=16 and 1+6=7 the number of Netzach, meaning victory. The value of the word Netzah נצח, is 148, 1+4+8=13 the value of the words אחד meaning unity and אהבה meaning love, both of which are qualities of the planet Venus that is allocated to Netzach. If we add 1+3 we obtain 4 which equals 10. 1+2+3+4, and ten is a return to unity. Moznaim, מאזנים, the Hebrew word for the astrological sign Libra also equals 148, and Venus is the planet ruling this sign.

Remember, astrological bodies are announcers of elemental energy. They are not that energy. They are signs in the sky that denote what is occurring in your environment and because you are a part of your environment, also within you. The points of the hexagram assigned to the planets are usually seen as the seven planetary sephiroth on the Tree of Life (see diagram 1-10).

However, for astral experiences, when you are traveling to the plane of the energy, it is more appropriate to apply the paths allocated to these planets, rather than the Sephiroth, as will be explained in what follows.

The Elohim are especially associated on the Tree of Life with the seventh Sephirah Netzach, meaning victory. With this meaning we deduce that seven is the number of overcoming adversity and achieving victory. Netzach has the planetary attribution of Venus, the astrological symbol which embraces the whole Tree of Life (see diagram 1-11). Therefore, by applying the Elohim to Netzach, the statement is being made that the Elohim entities manifest when a state of wholeness and harmony is achieved.

Consulting the color scale for the world of Briah on the Tree of Life, we discover that Netzach is green. This is the center of the color spectrum harmonizing the extremes of blue and red. The numerical value of Elohim, when spelled in Hebrew is, 86, 8+6=14[xxiv]. The 14th path of the QBL is ד, meaning door, and is assigned the planet Venus. The tarot card allocated to this path is the Empress and the color of this path is also green.

Returning to the number seven we find that the seventh letter of the Hebrew alphabet is ז meaning sword. It has the tarot attribution of the Lovers, whose interpretation is intuitive ability[xxv].

# Howling at the Sky

The sword in the QBL is the symbol of the Lightening Flash down the Tree of Life, 1-12. It creates the ten sephiroth. It is the sword that carves form out of primordial chaos. The Elohim, not appearing until a state of synthesis has been achieved, are therefore representative of an energy manifesting to transform that synthesized state into a new phase of being, through the action of the sword[xxvi].

Using the Garden of Eden to represent a synthesized state, Adam and Eve are the balanced condition of opposites, the fire and water triangles that make up the hexagram, diagram 1-08, and the Elohim are the transforming principle of the serpent[xxvii]. Adam and Eve are twin poles of energy. וד value 11 is the positive pole and וב value 9 the passive pole[xxviii]. When in balanced[xxix] disposition they manifest אור value 208, the light of open day. This manifestation is symbolic of an individual achieving dimensional interface[xxx] and becoming a resonator. The traditional term of Holy Guardian Angel is also referred to as Augoeides which is derived from the Greek word *augos*, meaning morning light, symbolic of the dawn of consciousness. When we can attune ourselves to resonate at specific frequencies and achieve dimension interface at will is when we receive our tuition by the Elohim. Ability to comprehend and act on this teaching will determine how much in the image of the Elohim we are made[xxxi].

The flaming sword that prevents Adam and Eve from returning to the garden after their enlightenment, achieved by passing through the gate of opportunity, symbolizes that one can not go back and change the past. However, one can use the past to impact on the future. This illustrates that the flaming sword of the past must be picked up and become the sword of the Lightening Flash to create the future.

The Elohim are the evolutionary process within the duration of existence, said to have made man in their own image. However, if the Elohim are a process within existence, then the Tree of Life is already complete for the Tree of Life is existence. This point is further endorsed by what is related in I Samuel 28:13 where the woman of Endor tells Saul, " I saw the Elohim ascending out of the earth." The earth is the sephirah Malkuth, the physical universe and the body of man. Therefore the Elohim are better represented as being elemental powers that are the forces of nature. We are made in the image of the Elohim when we are empowered with elemental energies. Once empowered, we can exercise our ability to transform[xxxii] by confronting adversity to rise out of the sphere of Malkuth, the material universe. This theory can be tested by studying diagram 1-13 and the titles High Priest כהן הגדול and High Priestess כהנת הגדול. High Priest כהן הגדול has the numerical value of 123 or if נ is taken as final 773, High Priestess כהנת הגדול has the numerical value of 523. 123 = 6 and so relates to the sephirah of Tiphareth and 523 = 10 which relates to the sephirah Malkuth. In studying diagram 1-13, we see that the High Priest is allocated to the Tiphareth of Yetzirah and the High Priestess to the Malkuth of Briah. In this arrangement the two unite 123 +523 to equal 646 אלהים when מ is taken as final. Therefore when the High Priest and the High Priest unite to create synthesis the אלהים manifest and the Flaming Sword descends to create Assiah, the fourth world of the QBL.

    In the system of the QBL the nature of adversity is personified by entities known as Archons who are upholders of established order. The Archons are the rulers of the seven planetary spheres on the Tree of Life. They are the Moon, Yesod; Mercury, Hod; Venus, Netzach; Sun, Tiphareth; Mars, Geburah; Jupiter, Chesed; and Saturn as the sum of the three Supernals above the Abyss. Described as barriers to the rise of the human spirit, the Archons are often referred to as fallen angels. This attitude is the usual reaction we have when presented with a challenging situation; we view that challenge as evil or threatening. With this perspective we will not be permitted to climb beyond Malkuth.

# Howling at the Sky

Our way through adversity is by emulating the Elohim which requires that we sacrifice what we are and transform to new situations dictated by the Archons. By emulating the Elohim, we become dynamic functions of change, interaction and process. These are the qualities of the paths of the Tree of Life. If the Sephiroth are the descent of energy, symbolized by the Sword of the Lightening Flash, then the paths are the way of return, symbolized by the serpent, (see diagram 1-14). If we are to be made in the image of the Elohim, who are Force, we need to climb the paths of the Tree of Life that is the way of the serpent. In the story of the Garden of Eden, it becomes apparent that the Forces of creation, the life force, are the serpent making Adam and Eve in their image. IHVH יהוה, the emergence of the life force is tested by adversity to see if the present vehicle is worthy to climb the Tree of Life and be a function of future development (see diagram 1-14).

Returning to the source, the Sephirah Kether, we will be empowered to wield the sword of creation illustrated in diagram 1-12.

By studying the Elohim, the seven faces of force as elemental energies, we are better able to understand ourselves and be more than what we presently are. The Elohim are the life-force in synthesized action, symbolized by the hexagram and its center that is a figure of wholeness with the ability to change. The ability to change is an attribute of the paths and this is why the angles of the hexagram are allocated to the planetary paths, not the Sephiroth, when traveling to the planes of elemental energy. When bringing energies to you, as in evocation, the traditional association is appropriate because the energies are materializing and becoming things which are qualities of the Sephiroth.

You can begin a study of the Elohim by consulting the color

scales of the QBL.  Meditate on the colors of the paths referred to the planets, to deduce the relationship between them and the forces operating in nature, of which they are announcers.  As an example, the color of Mars is red which easily corresponds to the elemental energy of fire, the color of the dried up earth during the heat of summer.  Other colors are not quite so easily allocated but it is a valuable exercise to play with them and their relationship as they relate to you a microcosm of the universe.

    In understanding the Elohim, we are made whole and manifest the hidden light of gnosis, the knowledge symbolized by our becoming aware of the eighth point of the hexagon. The manifestation of the eighth point occurs by a shift in consciousness and is symbolized by our shift in perspective. When looking at the hexagon and seeing it transform into a cube, we are revealing what was previously hidden (see diagram 1-15). This is a function of the serpent.  What is revealed is the point behind the center point of the Sun, which is assigned to the star Sirius.  With a change in perspective, we are empowered with the knowledge that the center is a corner, just like the other seven. Realization of the eighth point represents the birth out of one state of being into another.  It is the expression of life breaking out of  its confinement in wholeness, represented by the hexagon, and an awakening into a cube which offers the potential for wider experience.

    This change of perspective is a dynamic function illustrated on the Tree of Life by the path of ℶ whose tarot attribute is Death. The word death is misleading if we interpret it as being an end instead of realizing that there is no death, only transformation.  It is upon this path that the awakening of the hidden light of gnosis, represented by the hidden point of the cube in the hexagon, occurs.  This is demonstrated in the machine of the hexagram where the LVX signs are performed. *See chapter Basic Machines*

# Howling at the Sky

*of Attainment: The Machine of the Hexagram.*
The LVX, signs in conjunction with the god names of Isis, Set and Osiris, are utilized in the machine as a dramatization of the process of changing perspective. This moving from one state of awareness to another illustrates the process of metamorphosis.

The mourning of Isis is due to the loss of vitality brought on by wholeness which has become stagnant. This is the sign of the practitioner who has diligently worked the machines in *The Black Book of the Jackal* to create the circuits necessary for channeling the energies that will be released in Part III. It is paramount that we move forward to charge these circuits if we are not to dry up and die. The body posture for this sign is an upright cross symbolizing rigidity.

Set is the triumphant re-emergence of the life force after its confinement, bringing the excitement of future possibilities. The body posture now assumes the form of the diagonal, representing action, the crossing principle. The arms and legs are thrown out creating a double letter v, an x[xxxiii], between the arms of the previous cross. It represents a state in between, a quality of the paths, and Daath, the twilight realm. It is a symbolic gesture of entering unknown territory and new life experience.

Osiris slain and risen represents a vehicle which has successfully channeled life and has transformed from one state of being into another. With the arms folded across the breast and the head hung down on the chest the sign is demonstrating looking inward for the seed of the future. This sign combines elements of the previous two. The legs are together symbolizing rigidity and the arms are crossed across the breast symbolizing that the once unknown territory, entered symbolically by the previous sign, is now known and integrated within the self. It is a symbolic gesture of arrival and symbolizes what was once unknown is now known.

The LVX signs as a whole are Latin for light. This word aptly describes the process of the machine of the hexagram. If we convert LVX[xxxiv] into a number we obtain 65, L=50, V=5 and X=10. Sixty five in Hebrew is the number of אדני, ADNI, meaning My Lord. The name ADNI is generally recognized traditionally as being one's personal Holy Guardian Angel, referred to in this work as dimension interface. The process described above reveals the hidden aspect of the true self which has been concealed beneath the world of appearances that is the personality. If we add six and five we obtain eleven, the number of Daath.

The seven original gods of the ancient Egyptians were attributed to the seven stars of the Great Bear, the constellation that circumambulates the Northern Pole during the course of a year. These seven original gods of ancient Egypt were, Sebek, crocodile; Shu, lion; Iu, ass; Seb, goose; Taht, ibis; Apuat, jackal; Kabhsenuf, hawk[xxxv]. Experiment by assigning these zoomorphic images to the color scales allocated to the Elohim provided earlier, to expand your understanding of elemental energy.

The Pole Star, around which the constellation of the Great Bear rotates, is appointed to the god Anup, a jackal-headed deity who is an aspect of the god Anubis. Anubis, to the ancient Egyptians, was a guide through the underworld. This is an interesting correlation to the Pole Star, being a guide to travelers in the northern hemisphere for centuries. One of the titles of Anubis was Tepy-dju-ef, meaning "He who is upon his mountain," an epithet that evokes the image of Anubis watching from the heights, the Pole Star.

The stars of the constellation of the Great Bear make up the entity of the Great Mother, the hippopotamus God Taweret, and the stars individually, the seven original Gods, are her seven aspects. In its movement, this constellation completes a cycle representing wholeness and constitutes a year. The catalyst,

# Howling at the Sky

which marks the beginning and end of this cycle, is the rising of the star Sirius. It is the emergence into a new state of being symbolized by a new year. The star Sirius is in the constellation of Canis Major. Some authorities thus attribute to it the name Dog Star. However, I suggest the name Dog Star is given because of its similarity in energy to that of the Pole Star. The constellation of Canis Major then derives its name from being the location of the Dog Star, Sirius. Both stars, the Pole and Sirius, are openers of existence, the Pole Star macrocosmic, aeonic and Sirius microcosmic, annual. The image of dog or jackal is therefore the symbolic attribute of the act of opening or bringing into existence[xxxvi].

    Eight is the sun behind the sun, Sirius the opener of the year, the first born of the mother, the mother's son, the god Set[xxxvii]. For the duration of the cycle, Set has been invisibly incubating but now manifests as an expression of life into a wider theater of experience. This action is represented in the tarot card of the Chariot that corresponds to the eighth Hebrew letter ה. The event is equivalent to our receiving the light of gnosis, the realization of expanded possibilities and the rush of enthusiasm.

    The original mother, who is the constellation of the Great Bear, has completed a cycle providing an enclosure for the emergence of greater experience. This cycle creates a place of incubation and synthesis that can be represented by the god Isis. This image equates with the sphere of Netzach from the QBL. Isis is the mother from whom the imminent future will be born. Isis is the god of an individual year created by one revolution of the original eternal mother of all, who is the constellation of the Great Bear. As such, Isis represents a transient vehicle that exists so that something more might develop. She is the intermediate state between one act of originality and another.

    The energy represented by the birth of Set is the catalyst

of adversity because the act of doing or being something challenges that thing to exist. If it succeeds, it is worthy and proceeds to the next test or initiation. Set is the representation of the unknown future whose abode is the desert, a place where anything can happen that is as yet devoid of life. It is the adventure zone, better known as life and living, a dimension of unrestricted possibility. All you have in the future is what you bring into it; therefore your future is tainted by the baggage of your past that you carry with you. It has been said that your future is what you choose to make it. Set represents the breaking out of the mold of make-believe safety with nothing but the elemental energies of what you fundamentally are. This principle is symbolized outwardly by the cross within the square that creates depth out of flatness (see diagram 1-16). It is the tetrahedron of fire which is the reaction of life to restriction: friction[xxxviii]. It creates and destroys simultaneously and is a symbol of action[xxxix]. The secret encrypted by this figure is the double cube whose side elevation is the sigil of Set. When you look beyond appearances, you realize that the square and the cross are the base of the double cube and the diagonal root six which empowers you to travel between worlds, the Merkabah (see diagram 1-17). Therefore the sigil of Set, (see diagram 1-19), is the gate of entrance to the Merkabah, which is the double cube.

The square and cross are duplication and can be assigned to the god Horus. The double cube is an evolutionary leap where the status quo of duplication is transcended by the action of the rebel, the god Set. Horus is natural childbirth, as duplicating and propagating the known order. Set is a symbol of unnatural childbirth where original life breaks out and destroys the outmoded vehicle of its incubation. The significance of Set being the first born, is that he is the first born into a new reality,

# Howling at the Sky

different from that of his origin. Horus, as duplication on the other hand, represents the maintaining of established circumstances, such as that of state, society, family, religion or perpetuation of ego. All resurrection gods can be allocated to this position. Set is the rebel because, by initiating original circumstances, he cannot be reborn as he is always original. Set is the shadow cast when we receive the light of dimension interface[xl].

These concepts may sound harsh to our human sensitivities if we are programmed to believe that the only way to overcome adversity is through brute force. However, there are many ways to overcome obstacles such as that dramatized by Alexander the Great and the Gregorian Knot. The life-force expresses itself and experiences existence in infinite ways. It is sad that we in our present state look at adversity as bad rather than challenging.

To a magician, the name of a God is a formula, which if understood is a key that can unlock a gate to the energy represented by that name. The names of gods are ciphers that can be deciphered by anyone who wishes to be involved in the adventure of life. Gods are not to be worshipped. Their names are dynamic formulas and principles, the understanding of which empowers one with the energy represented by a specific formula.

A study of the ancient Egyptian *Book of the Dead* or, to use its correct translation, *The Book of Coming Forth by Day*, reveals that one must know the names of the gods who guard the portals of the underworld if one is to pass through them[xli]. It is commonly assumed that the traveler passing through these realms is deceased. However, I suggest that the term deceased is symbolic of representing an unenlightened individual, one who is not aware of their full potential. This book is not so much concerned with preparing for life after death but rather for enlightening oneself for successful existence in the future. By passing through the seven Arits[xlii] you unlock the barriers that restrain who you really are. Successful passage through these gates releases your true self from the bondage of ignorance that it might participate in the external world, the Adventure Zone.

In chapter CXLVII[xliii] of *The Book of Coming Forth by Day* is provided an account of this process of passage[xliv]. This chapter is particularly important because it is of an early period and therefore less tainted by dynastic influences. I would suggest that you study and experiment with the instructions provided in this chapter to seek correlation's between it the Elohim and the Archons. In *The Black Book of the Jackal,* I have provided machines and astral examples for making this passage. The machines are also provided in Part IV of this work.

To know the name of an energy is to understand its formula and be empowered with its essence so that you can pass through the portal it guards and experience environment. The symbolism of the portal is that it is a door opening into a new aspect of adversity. The doors are commonly illustrated as having the proportion of the double square which is one face of the double cube and the double cube is the vehicle of transformation, the Merkabah, the energy represented by the god Set.

One way of understanding the formula of these energies is through the practice of assumption of energy terra-forming[xlv]. Energy terra-forms are totems of Nature Powers, which are transforming principles. I should make it clear that when you invoke or evoke an energy you are not worshipping it. What you are doing is channeling your consciousness down the avenue of an energy so the specific energy will desire to temporarily inhabit the place you have made for it. The place, which is the consciousness of the magician, is formed so as to encourage that particular energy to want to inhabit you. This is achieved by

# Howling at the Sky

bringing together correspondences that are in tune with the energy in question. The decor of the temple, the circle and the clothing of the magician should all correspond to the attributes of the specific energy that is to be evoked.

After the preliminary banishing machines have been performed, the appropriate incense of the energy is lit. The magician now appeals to an energy to inhabit the self. You appeal, meaning making your consciousness as attractive[xlvi] to that energy as possible. You are not begging as in popular religion, you are fabricating yourself into an appealing environment so that the summoned energy will want to inhabit you.

Magic is not religion. Magic is a system of personal experience with energy and energy is another name for god. Religion should not seek to enslave or encourage fanaticism; its way is not the only way. It should encourage the realization of individuality and the expression of self in its participants. It should provide a framework and coherent reference system whereby its members can come to an understanding of themselves. Dimensional interface[xlvii], or in traditional magical terminology, conversation with one's Holy Guardian Angel[xlviii], is the beginning of one's true life path, either within the structure that manifested it or outside that structure. Dimensional interface is not an end but a beginning!

# Roger Williamson

## Howling at the Sky

# The Shadow Star
**Set**[xlix]
*Aspiration of life for original expression.*
*Carries the bloodline of the Mother[l].*
*The animal response to raw instinct, the drive to ride the natural cycle of the hunter and the hunted.*
*Following one's true life course that is observed by others as you using whatever means necessary to succeed.*
*The ability to take the wave of original opportunity.*
*Cold intellect when observed from an emotional standpoint.*

יהוה[li]
*The unpronounceable name of God from the Old Testament of the Bible.*
*Being unpronounceable, it parallels the symbols of the puzzle and the perpetual mystery of life.*
*This name is a combination of contradictory aspects that equate with opposition.*

Reference to the chapter QBL will be useful in elucidating the ideas expressed in this chapter.

Dimensional interface is first consciously achieved in the sephirah of Tiphareth whose planetary attribution is the Sun. In diagram 1-08 we see that the Sun is allocated to the center of the hexagon. With a change in our perspective we come to the realization that the hexagon is a cube and that behind the corner allocated to the Sun is a hidden corner, its shadow, diagram 1-20. This corner is allocated to the star Sirius that is the star of Set and the sephirah Daath. When this point is realized by our change in perspective, a whole new set of rules and dynamics come into play.  This is the quality of the energy represented by the stellar body of Sirius, which brings knowledge and conversation with one's Holy Guardian Angel[lii].

The nature of the energy represented by Set and its Hebrew equivalent יהוה is a synthesis of opposing qualities.  The name יהוה is a formula of action describing a process of controlled change and development which by definition cannot be a tangible thing or state of being.  In this respect it is equated with the paths of the Tree of Life and not the Sephiroth.  On first examination this appears to contradict the allocation of the name יהוה to the Sephiroth as described in the chapter QBL.  However, in that example you will observe that the name is not allocated to a single Sephirah.  Study reveals that when the name יהוה is applied to the Sephiroth it is divided amongst the contradictory qualities of the four Sephirah: Chokmah, Binah, Tiphareth and Malkuth[liii] (see diagram 1-21).  The division is illustrating that a process of development down the Tree of Life is achieved through these diversified aspects.  It emphasizes that the basis of all things, symbolized by the Tree of Life, is change and development.

Set and יהוה are god names representing the same energy.  In Egyptian mythology, Set is the God of the desert[liv] and it is יהוה who appears to the Hebrews in the desert.  In both instances this energy, Set/ יהוה, is the emergence of enthusiasm for life when presented with adversity, symbolized by the desert.  The desert is the place of hardship and testing where the inaction of complacency is overcome.  The Old Testament of the Bible is a chronological account of a race of people being incessantly tested to ascertain if they possess the necessary attributes to continue to the next challenge.  This has a correlation to industries' systems of quality control that do their utmost to guarantee the reliably of their products.

# Howling at the Sky

The wanderings of the Hebrews through the desert was an evaluation by their creator to insure their reliability as part of the creator's enterprise. The action of this energy is dual in nature and duality is a quality of the paths. The paths are where we are educated to understand the formulas for unlocking the puzzles of the Sephiroth, the challenges to our ignorance. This activity can equate with our own voluntary actions to grow and be more than we are. If we persevere, through the hardships of achieving our dreams and objectives then these dreams and objectives have a right to exist.

Set/ יהוה is the impulse of life's enthusiasm for original experiences, tested by the deserts of adversity that are the Sephiroth.

The challenges at the gates of the Sephiroth are an evaluation of their merit to exist. Set/ יהוה as the life force emerges and in so doing evokes its contradiction, opposition. These two qualities are one energy. They rise simultaneously as tests to each other's worthiness to exist. This dynamic is the principle of inversion which is the expression of "as above, so below" and that nothing can exist without its opposite. To some, what is being said might be interpreted as life being a procession of hardships. However, if due meditation is given to the Tree of Life it will be revealed that this is not the case.

Our first test is in the sphere of Malkuth where our ability to deal with the adventure of everyday life will be evaluated. Success achieved here, the ability to change our perspective[iv] to life's physical challenges, will allow us to move onto the sphere of Yesod, the astral realm and from there to Hod, the sphere of the reasoning mind. What is achieved through successfully overcoming an adversity is that our perspective toward it is changed. It is no longer painful and a true initiation is achieved for that particular sphere when it becomes an opportunity.

This can be illustrated by the behavior of a form that has achieved wholeness through experience, that now needs to transform, not recreate[lvi], if it is to continue as a vehicle of life. This is the action of moving from one state of being to another. Try working through each of the sephiroth of the Tree of Life from Malkuth to Kether to evaluate your ability to deal with the adversity offered by each of them. The paths leading from a specific sephirah offer clues to the energies required to synthesis and transform that sephirah within yourself and your relationship with the outside world.

To return to the example of Malkuth, we see in diagram 1-03 that three paths lead upward from this Sephirah. The path of ת value 400, the path of ש value 300 and the path of ק value 100. If we add these three letters we obtain 800, the value of the letter פ when it appears at the end of a word. The tarot card assigned to this letter is the Tower, which represents an image of breaking free from bondage or outmoded thoughts and ideas. The meaning of this letter is mouth, and you should meditate on this to further elucidate the concepts being expressed here. Eight hundred is also the numerical value of the Hebrew word קשת, meaning bow. With this interpretation we might say that our successful understanding of Malkuth empowers us with the vehicle of the bow, which can fire the arrow of our aspiration up the Tree of Life. The better our understanding of the bow and its use, the more likely is our arrow to escape the gravitational pull of Malkuth. Acquisition of the arrow for the bow is achieved later; meditate on the Tree of Life and its correspondences to see where this might occur. Another interpretation of the bow is that it is the Rainbow of Promise, peace after the storm or a tied ribbon that conceals a gift.

In the QBL combined contradictory aspects are a characteristic of the Supernals, the Sephirah Kether, Chokmah and

# Howling at the Sky

Binah, expressed through the action of Daath, a Sephiroth which according to the QBL does not exist. What the QBL means by this statement is that Daath, the action of the Supernals, is equivalent to the paths of the Tree of Life. This non-existent quality is an attribute of the paths because they are transitions from one state of being to another[lvii]. When the worlds of the Tree Of Life come together in a specific arrangement Daath does appear (see diagram 1-22). This demonstrates that when the worlds of the Tree Of Life interact with each other another dimension manifests. This is comparable to dissecting a human body. You can study and analyze the body's parts and qualities, but when they come together in correct synchronization life appears, that indefinable quality that is not the parts of the body. This is Daath.

    The symbol of the Supernals is a combined square and cross that create the tetrahedron of fire which is the reaction of life to restriction (see diagram 1-16). This tetrahedron is a correspondence of the 31$^{st}$ path of the Tree of Life. The Hebrew letter of this path is ש, Shin, meaning tooth, and is the letter assigned to the element of fire, the fire of the pure divine energy. Its numerical value is 300, which in Hebrew spells the words Ruach Elohim, meaning the Spirit of God. This is the fire experienced by the Hebrew patriarchs when encountering God during their wanderings in the desert. The tarot card assigned to the path is Judgement, meaning the taking of an irreversible step. After taking this step, things can never again be what they once were.

    You can see from a study of the letter ש that it is surmounted by three Hebrew י, Yods. The Hebrew letter י has a value of ten. The letter ש therefore is crowned by the value of 30. Thirty is the number of the Hebrew letter ל, Lamed, meaning ox-goad, associated with the astrological sign of Libra, meaning balance. Therefore we see that this fire is expressed in guiding by balanced action.

The god Set has red eyes and red hair, symbols of fire and the bloodline of the original mother. The mother is the first form to issue from the void and the physical attributes of Set depict that he is the first born of the mother, continuing the bloodline of originality. The desert symbolizes a form that has achieved wholeness through integration of opposites and is an image of the mother. It needs to transform if it is to continue to the next stage. The desert is a symbol of the square, wholeness, and Horus as the diagonal is the outward transformation of the desert square into a new figure. The diagonal, symbolized by Horus, is the crossing principle and equates with the image of the crossroads where an individual makes his pact[lviii] with supernatural forces[lix]. It is here that initial enthusiasm will agree to doing anything to get what it wants. The supernatural forces are Set[lx] who manifests when one realizes that the square is the base of the double cube and that the diagonal is in reality the geometric function root six which catapults one into a new reality (see diagrams 1-16, 1-17, 1-18).

When suddenly transported into a new reality, the self has the choice to adapt or die. The desert square of wholeness is devoid of duality. Where there is no duality there is no life. It is only through the action of the crossing principle, the paths of the Tree of Life, that life manifests. The crossing of the desert square creates life. Many will attempt the crossing but few will succeed. However, those that do succeed will insure that the following generations will be that much stronger. The successful provide a base for more challenging situations. Stamina and guile are qualities of a successful life vehicle that makes the crossing through crisis. The figure of the square and cross conceal three-dimensional reality. In crossing the desert we become alive and enter an environment where we are offered the opportunity to

# Howling at the Sky

transform ourselves to exist in a new set of circumstances.

The degree to which we adapt determines the degree of our initiation. Magical groups when developing a degree system of advancement would do well to bear this in mind if they wish their members to be self-empowered instead of subservient. The objective of a group, it should be remembered, is to empower its members with individuality. We admit that we can be more than we are and accept the challenge that adversity offers: to transform.

The first requisite is that we wish to participate in life and be adventurous. Next we determine the strength of our commitment by preparing ourselves for the task. This is probably where most of us are weeded out. The degree of accomplishment of this stage is determined to what degree we pursue the work laid out in *The Black Book of the Jackal*, or any other system of preparation you feel drawn to.

As you begin the work of preparation, you will probably find that friends and acquaintances will endeavor to detract you from your chosen course. This is a natural phenomena and should encourage you to continue. It is witnessed time and again as individuals exert themselves to expand their horizons and step beyond their social circles. Others within the circle often see this as a threat to their own security. What is really occurring is that others are resentful of your attempts to expand yourself because they don't want to make the effort. They believe that it is easier to drag others down to their level than to make the effort to climb out of where they are. This attitude has been popularized with the interpretation of traditional myths. Any superficial perusal of many popular myths or fairy tales encourages one to believe that the weak will succeed. This has been a deliberate deception encouraged by those in authority to encourage subservience. It appeals to the instinct within us for easy living, an exile from the adventure of being alive, that is premature death.  The weak will not succeed because life will not allow it[lxi].  If we are to continue as a species we need to reintroduce vitality back into our myths and belief systems.  The continuing popularity of adventure movies is a demonstration that we subconsciously desire vitality to emerge into our lives and they speak to the dormant energies within us to express themselves.  For a few short hours we are thrown into life by these movies and when they finish it is sad that we return to sleep.

In the story of Set and Osiris from ancient Egyptian mythology it has become the accepted view to judge Set as a cruel antagonist and something to be avoided.  This is because the cosmic principles of development, represented by the gods, have been degraded into human emotions that cling to the world of safety.

In this story Osiris is invited to a party by his brother Set.  While there, Osiris is tricked by Set into being entombed in a chest that is dumped into the Nile river, the Nile river being equivalent to the current of life.

I would suggest that in this scenario Set is offering Osiris the opportunity to travel between worlds.  Set is the catalyst for Osiris to enter the continuing adventure of life by inviting Osiris into the chest.  The chest is the geometric figure of the double cube containing the function of the root six which is the energy of traveling between worlds (see diagram 1-18).

The story is a symbolic representation of the life-force awakening into a vehicle to test the vehicles worthiness to continue its existence.

Osiris as an expression of the life-force that has reached its fullest expression in a particular form.  This can be compared to the completion of a cycle like the cycle of the year, with a new year emerges new life.  His entombment in the perfect geometric

# Howling at the Sky

shape of the double cube, which contains the root six, demonstrates that Osiris has reached a stage of development so complete and whole that in its present form there is nowhere else to go. If the life-force expression of Osiris is to continue there is only one action available: transformation. The Osiris vehicle must be transformed into a new and better expression of life to experience new levels of existence. The vehicle must travel between worlds, which is achieved by the geometric function of root six.

The transformed manifestation of Osiris is Horus, an image which is a vehicle better able to combat the adversity offered by Set. The action of root six initiated Osiris into the form he must assume if he is to combat and overcome adversity.

Observe that in this story the human component is Osiris. It is as though Osiris represents humanity in total as the wholeness of completion. This wholeness is transformed by the elemental powers of the zoomorphic images of the Gods, representatives of the forces of nature, expression of the current of life. Osiris re-emerging as the zoomorphic image of Horus demonstrates that we need to be a part of life to ride it.

There is another way to look at the results of this transformation.

The successful overcoming of adversity manifests the mark of courage in the vehicle that has achieved it. This is seen by those who have not attained this mutation as adversity. This mark of courage is the mark of Cain.

The challenged has become the challenger.

Horus can be attributed to Sirius if the energy represented by Sirius is only duplication, as exemplified as one year following on another. Set is synonymous with Lucifer, who is the Herald Star Sirius that announces the catalyst of a new year, representing the stepping into the unknown future of infinite possibilities. Sirius is a fitting symbol of duality because it announces the death of the old and proclaims the arrival of the new. It is the star of Set because it is initiating an original current born out of the ashes of the old order and therefore partakes of the symbolism of the phoenix. Lucifer is the light of gnosis that is bestowed upon those who, having completed a cycle, step out into the dark of an unknown territory with the illumination of experience. This unknown territory is symbolized as the beginning of a new year that is not just a duplication of its predecessor.

The symbol of the chest is that of the double cube containing the root six. This is the key to traveling between worlds (see diagram 1-18). The entrance to this figure is the Lucifer Sirius sigil, (see diagram 1-19), Lucifer and Sirius being the dynamic principle of creation.

The tomb as a symbol of the double cube brings one to birth in a new environment and a new environment demands that we adjust and transform if we are to exist in its atmosphere.

Set/ יהוה is the reaction of life against complacency that simultaneously manifests opposition to its emergence. By evoking this energy we manifest change and resistance to change, our reaction to which will decide our fate. This action is illustrated in the tarot card of the Devil where we see the light of illumination being offered to the figures at the bottom of the card. The light of the torch allows the figures to see that they are held in bondage, illustrated by the chains which restrain them, and to see their jailer who representing adversity is the challenge they must overcome to be free. The amount of illumination they receive, symbolized by the torch, determines the quantity of adversity they become aware of. This is why too much illumination received too quickly can destroy our dreams because we become aware of what we must overcome. So when setting ourselves goals, we need insure that they are challenging yet

# Howling at the Sky

obtainable if we are not to despair and give up at the first hurdle. The Hebrew letter assigned to this card is ע meaning eye, a symbol having a correlation with light and the ability too see. Its numerical value is 70[lxii] and when spelled in full עין, has the value of 130[lxiii].

    The degree to which we wish to live will be mirrored in the degree of opposition we encounter. The better we prepare ourselves then the better we will be able to deal with the opposing forces we are presented with. Adversity exists to challenge new life to see that it is worthy to exist. Without this challenge there is no life. This is the curse of man, that we seek safety, a state that does not exist. Seeking to be tested makes us stronger and more adaptable to life's continuing drive into the unknown future. The story of Set and Osiris is the act of our awakening to a state of complacency when we have become comfortable with our achievements.

Either we will go forward and change or we will wither and die because we are unable to deal with new environments that will inevitably be offered to us. However much we would like to believe we can prevent change, we cannot. The concept of safety is an illusion created by those who offer to protect you, so they can inevitably control you by the promise of escape from adversity. Comfort, the result of this escape, is the illusion that will eventually deprive you of your will. This scenario is perpetuated by the actions of religions, politicians and big businesses which offer a freedom from decision making.

    The story of Osiris and Set is of birth and the continuation of a life-vehicle. In nature, life-vehicles are incessantly being tested to exist to see if they are worthy representatives of life. It begins at birth and ends at death when life departs to find a more suitable vehicle to express itself.

When we evoke Set/ יהוה we are saying we choose to live; we

have accepted that we are alive; we are a vehicle of life; and we accept the torch of individuality and accountability for our actions. It is with this torch that we enter the unknown land and with its light, Lucifer, bring to life that which had previously been without form. We accept the challenge of adversity. We choose to be tested. We choose to live.

# Howling at the Sky

## Summary

Magic is the ability to evoke and invoke natural energies for the pursuit of knowledge so that we can participate more fully in the adventure and mystery of life. It is personal contact with energy that leads us to the realization that life is ambiguous and provides us with the strength to be at ease in that ambiguity.

The preliminary work of magic is to gain an understanding of the self. Once this understanding is achieved, the magician can call on an aspect of personality that is a fitting conduit for a specific form of energy. The better the self is understood then the more precise and less diluted will be the energy channeled.

At this stage of understanding in the magicians development the magician can manipulate energies that are understood to use them as a vehicle to quest into wider ranges of experience. This is an ongoing process because magic is the technique that thrusts us into more diverse experiences so that the life force gains more insight.

What are these energies? I would say that like ourselves they are systems which are facets of the life force: the infinitely small and infinitely large existing in our dimension and also systems existing in other dimensions. As we call on their powers during magical ritual, I believe that they equally call on ours. In normal consciousness, their drawing on our energy by and large goes unnoticed but to the magically empowered individual these currents can be detected and if need be resisted. The individual, unable to resist, may fall victim to fatigue or sickness, while those possessing some insight into altered states of reality, but lacking the knowledge of its origins and laws may fall victim to madness. There is a specific way of arranging the worlds of the Tree of Life so as to manifest Daath, the gateway leading into other dimensions. The worlds when so arranged become the machine of the Merkabah. Like intermeshing gears, the worlds of the Tree engage to drive the Merkabah machine. In "On The Arrival Of The Machine And Its Mode Of Operation" I provide a dramatization of the machines appearance and a description of its components. When laying out a specific magic circle we are manufacturing a synthetic environment conducive for a specific energy to want to temporally occupy it so that we can communicate with it to better understand what it is and to draw into our own sphere of sensation its essence. The technique is vampiric and follows the cycle of the eater and the eaten. The circle will be a synthesis of our life experiences relating to the specific energy we wish to contact.

It is well to remember that parts of our own consciousness are also being drawn upon and called by the inhabitants of alien zones for use in empowering the denizens of these regions.

The powers on the QBL Tree of Life are the paths, ambiguity and mystery, the way of the serpent and not the sephiroth which are things, materialization of energy. Meaning, the sephiroth are things or states of being which give temporary form to rationalize energy; whereas the paths are measures of difference in that they are the powers of geometry, dynamic functions of change, commonly referred to as gods. We rationalize our experiences in a sephirah and then throw ourselves back into the mystery of the paths. The sephiroth need to be cracked open to release the pure energy of the paths. The spent, cracked open shell cases of the sephiroth then fall and become the Qlippoth. The strength of the Qlippoth is directionally proportional to our need for clinging to past programming and achievements. Sacrifice is the act of letting go of our past achievements and associations so that we are no longer tormented by them, the Qlippoth. They become fuel for the merkabah, the substance that will power it to voyage into infinite dimensions of experience.

# Howling at the Sky

In this day and age so many of us have removed ourselves from what is real.  We are encouraged to think and believe that life can be safe.  We need to realize that being born is dangerous and life is not safe - it is hazard.

Our first step therefore, should be to return our consciousness back to that of primordial man to  retrieve what we have lost.  It is to be thrown back into the primordial soup where we are reborn as angels with burnished wings.

# Roger Williamson

# Howling at the Sky

# Part II

# Roger Williamson

# Howling at the Sky

## Interlude

It was then that something mysterious occurred.

There is a quality that over the years, for no better reason than because I lack an adequate command of language to communicate its specific attributes, I have come to call z. I therefore stumble to explain it by saying it's an indefinable sense of expectancy, a something that disturbs me. I don't understand why this happens and understand less what it is. It wasn't until someone else said, "You know, that sense of expectancy you get, that feeling that anything can happen, those times when you sense that something intangible is about to occur that will drastically change your life for ever". It is one of those rare experiences that can only be explained to another if the other has undergone it. It is to relive an experience.

The catalyst of z could be a person, a physical accident, or an opportunity which suddenly presents itself demanding that your life be forever changed. I have encountered this quality z in so many diverse regions and environments around the globe. I have also discovered that it is not something that is restricted to a specific kind of atmosphere. I have encountered it in the busy populated boulevards of Paris. There, walking preoccupied, absorbed in my surroundings, I have experienced the sensation that a stranger might suddenly step out from one of the innumerable shadowed doorways or alleys.

In that magical environment of kaleidoscopic wet night air, spangled with incalculable stars of neon, a doorway mirrored the entrance into the labyrinth depths of my own inner being. Here was the arena of conflict where I could confront the shadowed stranger who was my jailer. The resonance of these two worlds would then spin within me the mystique of detachment and propel me into another reality where my jailer became my

# Roger Williamson

liberator through knowledge.

In quiet woods of England while standing solitary enveloped in the emanations of smells and colors of nature, I could hear its arrival as it was announced by the wind. An undulating wave of sound high in the limbs and foliage of the trees had become a vehicle bearing the message of the approaching event z. It might occur again at any unexpected time in a suburban park, a house or at a sea shore. It is a genius loci that resides invisible and unaffected by what occurs in its local. Patiently and passively it waits until, an intonation, set up by an approaching body in tune with its being, activates it into dynamic communication. It is a common energy, a single being that permeates the universe and emerges in myriad locations on planets, suns, galaxies and within the cool and protective darkness of infinite space. Each of its manifested locations is a mouth we can enter to be devoured so to experience the revitalization of the life force within us. It is a dare, a door of opportunity, a place of sacrifice, where we receive a command to lay down our achievements so that they can be the fuel to propel our revitalized selves into original realms of reality.
The arrival of the machine was such an event.

# Howling at the Sky

## On the Arrival of the Machine and its Mode of Operation
## A guided meditation into the adventure zone

I

On this particular morning I felt perfect calm and cohesion with the universe. I took my walk along a tree lined path leading down to a park infrequently visited by the local population. In this solitude, the power zones within my body reached out with prehensile outgrowths to mesh with their counterpart selves in the larger universe outside of myself. At this moment, I and the universe functioned as one organism. We were linked by subtle girders of electromagnetic pulse waves that resonated the fabric of my being in a euphoric symphony performed by the harmony of nature's philharmonic.

While in this state, I arrived at the lower end of the path where it opened out into a small tree enclosed area. There had once been a gate here, and although the gate itself had gone, the gnarled and rotted wooden posts still remained. As I put my arm out to lean on one of them, my hand brushed against something that felt like a piece of stiff cloth. Idly, I looked down to confirm my first impression that it was a piece of old fabric, but was sharply taken aback by the realization that it was an animal. Closer examination revealed that it was a dead bat nailed head down to the wooden post. Instinctively, I quickly lowered my hand and rubbed it against my trouser leg to remove any visible or invisible contamination.

My calm mood shaken, I gazed across the park. There was a mist that hovered several feet off the ground and parallel with it, giving the impression that the world was divided into that which was above and that which was below. Beneath, there was the vivid green grass, moist and over shadowed by the grayish tones of the mist. Through the haze, just above the tree line crowning the scene like a regent through the glazed luminosity of this mist frosted morning, the sun hovered like a dead orange thing. Traversing these two worlds, in the trees deep within the mist, crows called to their companions in invisible habitats.

As I gazed upon the apparent chaos of nature's flora in the surrounding trees, the leaves, branches and spaces in-between began to assume terrifying zoomorphic images in combinations that ebbed and flowed in and out of each other, from image to image. Wave upon wave of original random figures rose and washed over me to challenge my reasoning faculty's ability to comprehend them.

How long I remained in this mood, I don't know, but what seemed like hours was probably only seconds. I was pulled out of my other worldly mood when a movement from across the park caught my eye. As I took closer note of the distraction, I observed a young woman standing alongside a small shrub. Because of the mist, she assumed the dream like astral qualities of a pre-raphalite maiden: soft, delicate and one able to cause hallucination in her beholders. From where I stood, it was difficult to be sure of her age. Her hair was dark and full, falling in curls and tendrils like vines across her shoulders. She was very tall, I deduced, probably over six feet. After registering her height, what was most striking about her was the way she was dressed, for her apparel was far removed from the usual daytime conformity of suburbia. She wore a dress that had the appearance of being manufactured from a material of fluorescent aluminum foil. It wasn't so much that she wore the dress as it was that it was an apparition, like a holographic image, that hovered over her. It was then that I was suddenly taken aback realizing that she was the woman I had met over lunch several weeks previously in the Bell and Cannon . I wondered if she

# Howling at the Sky

recognized me since she appeared to be keenly staring in my direction. As we continued to observe each other, she moved a hand to the back of her neck. She must have unclasped her dress, for it fell to the ground, leaving her entirely naked. Actually, now that I think about it, it wasn't so much that it fell, it was more like it disintegrated. Taken aback by this startling action, I at first looked away out of embarrassment. Looking into the powerful tangled undergrowth, I perceived a hare observing me with erect anticipating ears. We locked eyes as though in hypnotic trance until I made a nervous movement of my head, and so, quite suddenly, the hare turned and jumped off to become an invisible component in the world of the unseen.

Hesitantly, I returned my attention to the young woman. Her body had taken on the qualities of her dress, like an apparition created to conceal something beneath. What was beneath I couldn't determine, but I was inclined to believe it was not human, and possibly not even of this earth. The feral undulating movements of what was underneath her skin was akin to the ebbing and flowing of the primordial zoomorphic images I had witnessed earlier in the trees. As I continued to gaze upon her, the curves of her body, animated by the wild surging of what ever was within her, acted like the divine names on a medieval talisman charming the actions of my body like they would a spirit in magical evocation, and animated me into motion. I involuntarily ventured to walk in her direction, and as I did so, I discerned that her relationship to me maintained its initial distance. Therefore, as I approached the point where I had first cast eyes upon her, she had moved behind the bush and was hidden from my sight. I quickened my pace. When I arrived at the spot where I had last seen her before she became hidden by the bush, she was gone. I looked all around. Neither she nor the dress was anywhere to be seen, and I was left to wonder if she had ever existed.

I looked around the bush and then back across the park from where my walk had originated, but I couldn't see her, or any evidence that she had ever been there.

It was then that something caught my eye lying on the ground. It was a disk about ten inches in diameter. Picking it up, I found it to be very light and thought it to be constructed out of a cardboard like material. I assumed that the item was a mask because of a length of cord which was attached to either side. The construction however, denied the fact because of the omission of eye, nose and mouth apertures.

The outward image on the face of the mask was of a badly drawn, yet intriguing, goat's head. The primitive execution of its scrawled, broken crayon lines was tantalizing and hypnotic. It subconsciously encouraged me to make a deeper examination beyond what the outward artistic workmanship warranted. With closer scrutiny, I discerned that the face was actually the geometric figure of the pentagram. The lowermost point was the goat's beard, the two lower horizontal points its ears, the top two points its horns. As I casually fingered the mask, I felt drawn to turn it over and examine the inside. Here, upon a gray background, was an arrangement of circles and crescents in gold, red, blue, green, purple and yellow.

As I gazed upon the circles, they began to move and intermesh like gears in a machine. The figure took on a vampire like personality, sucking me into the heart of its being, impelling me to put the mask over my face.

II

When I emerged from the machine's embrace, it was dark. The night sky hung heavy with an overwhelming cacophony of stars that violently impelled themselves like a raging juggernaut into

# Howling at the Sky

my fragile consciousness. Vainly, I tried to draw coherence out of these celestial chaotic abnormalities in an effort to afford me some relationship to the cosmos. However, the nightmare of discord continued to maintain its suffocating anomaly, and the infinite possibilities offered by the stars gave no resolution to my questing cognizance.

How long I was subjected to this condition, I don't know. I do recall, that quite unexpectedly, the sequined black colossus that was the night sky melted like gelatin in water. The denizens of another dimension, as though entering by way of a back door, moved into and melded with my mind as unknown and uninvited guests.

At first, I assumed that the gate of the other dimension was in the sky, but now having had the time to reflect on the situation, I realize that my own inner turmoil, caused by the images on the inside of the mask, was the catalyst that opened the gate, breaching time and space. For an instant, as a star gate opened, the universe was folded and a leap of unfathomable proportion was achieved.

Further examination of the experience has made me realize that I am not the person I was; I am less, and yet, I am more. The part of me that passed through the threshold is lost, but what came out through the aperture, I have gained. There has been an exchange. Some form of other dimension consciousness has been spliced, or absorbed into my own, making me a hybrid. Since this occurrence, I have been afflicted by feelings of alienation. I am sure that these sensations originate from the alien intrusion and its feeling of disassociation in my consciousness. Therefore, the grafting of this intelligence into my own has not yet been fully accomplished, and we coexist as a dual personality. When I experience feelings of anxiety, I know that the entity or substance, or what ever it might be, is communicating with me in

# Roger Williamson

an endeavor to align my own sense of perspective with its own. It is pushing me into unfamiliar territory. It is endeavoring to get me to think like it. What for me is anxiety, is to it frustration at my lack of enterprise and daring when confronted by original and challenging situations. It is hungry for experience, adventure and growth; for, this is what feeds it. Does this now make me the unwitting host of a species incubating in me, waiting for its time to break out and populate our dimension; or, have I been uniquely bequeathed a gift of higher intelligence that will allow me to make a leap in consciousness. Is there a difference?

# Howling at the Sky

## A Brief Explanation of the Machine: Its QBL and Geometric Correspondences

The machine, diagram 2-01, is derived from a specific arrangement of the QBL[lxiv] Tree of Life which manifests the Sephirah Daath. See diagram 1-22 for the arrangement of the QBL in the four worlds.

For this machine, the trees of Atziluth, Briah and Yetzirah are used because they are the most refined qualities of the energies involved. The machine's impact will be actualized in the world of Assiah which is the adventure zone.

The relationship of the circles' dimensions to each other is derived from the squaring of the circle[lxv].

With this arrangement, a harmonic relationship is produced. The resonance,
generated by the conjunction of the Sephiroth Malkuth of Atziluth, Tiphareth of Briah and Kether of Yetzirah, is the Daath sphere.

From the diagram 1-22 it can be seen that the Yesod of Atziluth produces the Daath of Briah, and the Yesod of Briah generates the Daath of Yetzirah.

Note also in Atziluth the path פ, meaning mouth, allocated to the planet mars, aligns with the path ד, meaning door, allocated to the planet Venus, in Briah. This allocation is reflected in reverse between Briah and Yetzirah.

Also observe that the path ג of Assiah allocated to the High Priestess of the tarot connects to the Malkuth of Briah. Therefore it seems apparent that the High Priestess of Assiah is the Shekinah of the Malkuth of Briah. Meditate on the implications of these correspondences and the many other combinations that become apparent upon reflecting on diagrams 1-02, 1-03 and 1-21.

This arrangement demonstrates that the worlds of the QBL are

# Roger Williamson

intermeshed and not separate units acting independently. When the worlds synchronize with each other they become the components, like gears, that are the body of the Merkabah.
The worlds in this illustration can also be equated with dimensions. When the dimensions of height, width and depth come together and are understood the fourth dimension, imagination, is accessible.
Our adventures are as large as our ability to imagine.

## Part III
# Pandemonium

Capital city of demons built from underground precious metals founded by Mammon, the fallen angel.

# Roger Williamson

# Howling at the Sky

## Entering the Adventure Zone

The machine has arrived. If it is to be of any use, we need to understand its mechanism and how its action relates to our everyday lives. Becoming aware of the machine is our prize for traveling the underworld to discover our powers, Yesod and ה, and harnessing, these powers, Tiphareth and ס, so that we can free ourselves from the prison of dependence upon materiality and bogus promises of security and safety. This is not to say that materiality does not have its place. The material world is the Adventure Zone where we experiment, interact and grow along side and intertwine with other machines. It is the dimension in which the workings and energies of the other worlds of Atziluth, Briah and Yetzirah are realized into physical sensation. In it we should materialize our purest conception of the life force so that it can experience its optimum desire for diversity.

If we study diagram 3-01, we can see that in Malkuth of Yetzirah, our minds are connected to Assiah, the world of our physical sensations and environment.

In Tiphareth of Yetzirah, we are aligned to the Kether of Assiah and the Malkuth of Briah, the world of feeling.

In Kether of Yetzirah, we are connected to the Tiphareth of Briah and the Malkuth of Atziluth, the invisible world beyond sensation, thinking and feeling. Atziluth is some times referred to as the Invisible or Bornless Spirit[lxvi], meaning it is beyond the world of faculties and the ability to articulate. Looking at diagram 3-01, it can be seen that the most available vehicle of expression for Atziluth is through feeling: Briah and that mind, the world of Yetzirah, only remotely touches it through its most ethereal sephirah of Kether.

Yetzirah, our reasoning mind, is our everyday personality manifesting outwardly through Assiah. The nature of this personality will depend upon from which sephirah or sephiroth our reasoning mind functions. In its Malkuth, we are immersed in physical sensation and gratification of senses. In Tiphareth, we express ourselves artistically by rationalizing: Yetzirah; our feelings: Briah; into sensation or physical manifestation: Assiah. When we begin our journey our reasoning mind resides in Malkuth where we seek to find comfort and security in the physical world. Our first excursions from the world of appearances lead us to Yesod where we intermesh with the Daath of Assiah. This is the symbolic moon lit crossroads where we make our pack with supernatural forces; but, we never get what we thought we were going to get. This is because of the unseen currents, the harmonic sephirah of Yesod that is Daath of Assiah, that lurks on the path of ג in Assiah. It is after making our pact and falling into Daath that we gain knowledge of the circumstances operating in the shadowed moonlight. Here we come into the cycle of the protagonist of myth, who's initial adventures lead them into the underworld, where they acquire the knowledge[lxvii], resources and power required to fulfill their mission. The novice traveler, upon reaching Yesod of Yetzirah, will be drawn into Daath of Assiah and then down the path of ג, the High Priestess of the tarot who possess the astrological quality of the moon, back to where they began at Tiphareth/Yesod. This wheel[lxviii] will continue to turn until the adventurer has learned the lessons required to move further. Individuals who move from one system to another without comprehending or successfully completing the work of any one system are caught in this cycle. They run around in circles because they continue to fall down the same hole. Successful navigation here, earned through persistent work and an honest assessment of self, can earn the individual the keys of the underworld which is the harnessing of material forces. You control yourself through disciplines learned by

# Howling at the Sky

traveling the path of the Universe ת. A title of Yesod is Vision of the Machinery of the Universe[lxix]. Meaning, when consciousness is in Yesod it is resonating and in harmony with Daath of Assiah, the sephirah of knowledge, and observing how the material universe functions. It is to become the fruit of the QBL Tree Of Life in a self contained capsule, and to fall into a new realm of reality. It is a new realm of reality because our perspective has changed on how we view ourselves and the world we interact with because of experience. Using the movie 2001 as an example of this process, the black monolith, symbol of the unknown, is first discovered on the Moon which corresponds to Yesod, and when discovered, it connects with its counterpart the stargate in Jupiter[lxx] space. The next encounter with the monolith in Jupiter space projects David Bowman into the stargate and he then returns to Earth as the starchild[lxxi]. This scenario is symbolic of our first encounter with Yesod when we are drawn down into Daath, the stargate, and return to Earth, the world of Assiah. We are then back where we started but with knowledge, Daath, of the path and the vehicle which transported us. By this experience we should realize that we need to better understand the path and our vehicle so that we don't continue to rotate around the same sequence of life experiences. This requires discipline, a quality of the path ת.

In Tiphareth we earn the keys of the overworld through traveling the path of ס, the tarot card Temperance, because we learn how to blend the energies we acquired in the underworld. This is actualized through various forms of alchemy such as music, painting and other forms of creativity. It is creativity which unlocks the jail of material sensation and frees us to experience the worlds of Briah and Atziluth by manifesting an otherworldly quality within all manifestations of the mundane world. It is to become aware that all things and entities operate on all worlds of the QBL Tree Of Life . In Tiphareth of Yetzirah, the prince of Yetzirah unites with the Princess of Briah. This creates or realizes the Elohim[lxxii], and releases the sword of creation into Assiah. Meaning, that you create for yourself a new world view. See diagram 3-01 where the sephiroth of Kether of Assiah, Tiphareth of Yetzirah and Malkuth of Briah engage.

It is in Tiphareth that we achieve dimension interface because here we align with Malkuth of Briah and Kether of Assiah. These three worlds unite and interact upon each other to bring about a change in consciousness because the reasoning mind has become aware of something beyond itself and the body with which it has been interacting. I believe the achieving of dimension interface is experienced and related by some individuals as alien intrusion.

Tiphareth is the sixth sephirah and equates with the tarot card of the Hierophant. If you study the image of the Hierophant, whose letter is ו the sixth letter of the Hebrew alphabet, using The Rider Waite tarot deck, you will see these keys of the overworld and the underwold depicted at the feet of the central figure.

The four worlds of the QBL Tree Of Life illustrated in this work offers a myriad of correspondences and ideas that should be extracted by the adventurer for him/herself. When arranged in this way the worlds manifest the sephirah Daath, the sephirah which is supposed to not exist. However, we can see that Daath does appear when the QBL becomes a dynamic system when arranged as illustrated in diagram 3-01. Daath is that immeasurable something that appears when a system becomes alive and departs when a system dies. This means, when the worlds are realized as an integrated system working upon each other, they manifest that invisible something which is beyond quantification. It is sad how we notice it most when it departs, as in observing the body of a deceased friend or loved one, realizing that the indescribable something which we knew as this person is

# Howling at the Sky

no longer present. Death has occurred because the wheels of the worlds in this individual, once synchronized with each other, have become disengaged. The quality that was Daath has departed.
I hope this brief description of the dynamics of the QBL will encourage you to make your own inroads to the infinite worlds beyond appearances.

# Roger Williamson

# Howling at the Sky

## Draconian Architecture

If you have been performing the practices provided in The Black Book of the Jackal, you should be starting to become aware of the different facets of yourself. Knowledge of who and what you are builds your personal machine of attainment, the Merkabah. It is this that will empower you to become a conscious entity prepared to enter the vacuum of the future that is the Adventure Zone.

In this volume you learn how to fire your Merkabah machine so that you no longer have to tolerate being be a victim to life and society's values and circumstances. Now you are offered the opportunity to walk with the gods and dictate your own future assisted by your awakened intuitive faculties .

You can be anything you want to be if you want it enough. However, everything has its price. The question is, how much are you prepared to pay to get what you want. Before you answer, be sure that you know what it is you want.

We are perpetually being drawn into the vacuum of the future, the Adventure Zone. The better your understanding of the vehicle that transports you, yourself, the more likely you are to succeed.

Magic is power. Power over the self that gives you power over your environment.

If you have been diligently working the machines in The Black Book Of The Jackal, also included in Part IV of this work you should by now be seriously questioning the fundamental beliefs of what ever philosophy you grew up in. The object of this volume is to give you that final push into the abyss of self reliance. It is here that you will be yourself, nothing more and maybe not even that. Here is the sacrificial act. It is the investment of your achievements, the currency demanded for entering into the Adventure Zone.

# Roger Williamson

What follows is a system of personal attainment employed for developing expressions of individuality. There is no room for everyday personality beyond it being a vehicle for you to interact with what is outside of yourself. The personality is a mask that can put on and taken off at will. The nature of the mask depends on the operation you wish to achieve. If one is to be a conscious vehicle of life, the first sacrifice is to look beyond your personality and to experience for yourself what you truly are. It is to look beneath the mask and know the primal self that is common to all things. We and our world have a common source that is the residue thrown off by a star known as the Sun. Just like the Sun, the galaxy and the myriad of other galaxies and stars are all thrown off from one energy source. This is sometimes referred to as the Big Bang.

Who you are is not important and neither is humanity as a whole or any other species. Life is life and the vehicle of this energy is transient. Each is a plastic medium developed for experience. The quality of a vehicles existence is dependent upon its ability to express life. What this means is this anything that exists is not the end result of life's expression.

The preoccupation of humanity with its own sense of self-importance is an aversion to life. Life will resolve this state of affairs in its own way.

This statement may be misinterpreted as meaning one should not care about anything or anybody. This attitude misses the point. To understand this statement one must realize that everything is a part of the fabric of existence, each part no better or worse than another part. Our objective should be directed towards synthesis, so a leap of transformation may occur within ourselves and within the universe. In the present work the leap is achieved through the system of the QBL through the application of the Merkabah. Although the Merkabah is of QBL origin, I wish to demonstrate

# Howling at the Sky

there is a common underlying thread between the QBL and the mythology of ancient Egypt which harmonize into a coherent system of reference.

The gods of ancient Egypt and the power zones of transforming principles of the QBL are indelibly linked by association of common imagery.

For the people of the Nile valley, the inundation of the river was a new and original pulse of life released to transform their world, the land having attained a state of wholeness. This action equates with the change of perspective one experiences when seeing a three-dimensional form emerge from a two-dimensional geometric whole figure.

In the system of the QBL, the inundation is the lightening flash down the Tree of Life initiated by the appearance of Kether from out of the void. However, the correlation of the star Sirius in the QBL is allocated to Daath. This is because Daath is the first understandable expression of the Supernal Sephiroth above the Abyss. The rising of the star Sirius announced the emergence of the life source in ancient Egypt. The land having become barren was in a state of wholeness where all opposites were balanced out, symbolized by the square of the desert, the mother.

The rising of Sirius is the birth of the mother's son, the morning star, which fertilizes the valley of the Nile, the body of the mother, making the mother pregnant with new life. This new life can be one of two types. The mother can be fertilized by the energy of Horus to continue the previous world order and maintain the status quo of previous generations. Or the energy of Set can be realized and expressed as a new world order that rises from out of the ruins of the old to create original and unique life situations.

We all experience periods of complacency in our lives from time to time and these periods can be equated with the symbol of the desert. What has occurred at these times is we have achieved a state of wholeness. If this wholeness is not to regress into inertia we need to call on the energy, symbolized by the god Set, to take what we have achieved and invest it in the unknown future. This is the natural flow of nature. The alternative is to cling to what we have achieved and become inert. This path will lead us on a downward spiral which will eventually erupt in the explosion of the life force escaping its restriction to seek a more suitable expression for itself. This action of the life force is dramatized as the wrath of God, the result of life's escape from confinement within an outmoded vehicle which is no longer able to adapt. The world is full of the walking dead who have outlived their usefulness and are waiting to be recycled.

Lucifer, meaning morning star, is generally assumed to be Venus. However, I believe that Lucifer, the morning star, should be assigned to Sirius, which rises with the Sun to announce the inundation of the Nile. From this it can be construed that Set and Lucifer equate as a common energy principle, originality.

The Lucifer/Sirius sigil, diagram 1-19, contains the seed of the 3,4 and 5 triangle, diagram 3-02, whose proportions are the key to the Golden Section, *pi*, which is the function of harmonious creation.

The Lucifer/Sirius sigil is the key to the chariot of the Merkabah, defining it as a vehicle of natural unfoldment.

The 3,4 and 5 triangle is the proportion of the Great Pyramid at Giza whose side elevation is illustrated in diagram 3-03

The Egyptian hieroglyph for pyramid can be depicted as either diagram 3-04a or 3-04b[lxxiii].

The Egyptian hieroglyph for Sirius is depicted as either diagram 3-05a or 3-05b[lxxiv].

The Egyptian hieroglyph for earth is illustrated in diagram 3-06. Therefore in the hieroglyph for pyramid, diagrams 3-04a and 3-04b, we see that it can be interpreted as Sirius on Earth.

# Howling at the Sky

The Egyptian hieroglyph for Sirius is the same as that of tooth. Tooth in Hebrew is the letter שׁ that corresponds to רוח אלהים Spirit of God, because of them both having the same numerical value of 300. The geometric figure of the 31st path of the QBL allocated to the letter שׁ is the tetrahedron of fire (see diagram 1-16). The tarot card assigned to this path is Judgment.

What is being described is that Sirius partakes of the quality of fire. That it is the vitriol fire of alchemy. The hidden stone of the philosophers that burns through the veil of Isis and moves us into altered states of reality behind and beyond the known universe. In diagram 1-18, it can be seen that the root six lines converge and meet in the center of the square dividing the two cubes. This dividing square is the veil of Isis and it is here that the machine (diagram 2-02) operates. The interpretation of the tarot card Judgment endorses this for it is the taking of a definite and irreversible step. Once a leap in consciousness has been achieved life will never be the same.

This demonstrates that our ancestors were in possession of knowledge that has become forgotten or has been eradicated by conventional belief systems for their own ends.

To take this concept further we must return to the four worlds of the Tree of Life.

There is a common concept there are two sides to the Tree of Life, the Light side and the Dark side representing solar and lunar influences, reason and intuition, respectively (see diagram 3-07). The solar side is allocated to the god Horus and is the framework or circuit channeling the primal raw energy of the lunar side, allocated to the god Set. The lunar side is undifferentiated raw primal energy and assumes the form brought to it by the attitude of the person entering it, meaning our attitude to a situation when faced by adversity.

I suggest, however, that the Dark Side of the Tree, the raw

undifferentiated primal energy, is the power beyond Kether, the Tree above the Tree, rather than the concept of it being a reflection of the Tree described above.

To the magician in Assiah, the Tree of Yetzirah is the Dark Tree, raw primal energy, the unknown and the god Set.  The Light Tree is where he/she is, the world of Assiah representing the known and the god Horus.  Observe how Daath of Assiah, the Sirius Set sphere, connects with the Yesodic Lunar sphere of Yetzirah and that both spheres are shades of purple  (see the chapter, QBL and table 2).

The Egyptian hieroglyph for Sirius is diagram 3-04, the side elevation of the Great Pyramid whose proportion is based upon the Golden Section.  Observation of the side elevation of the pyramid gives the impression that it is a highway traveling into the sky.  This is our way of return to the infinite from where we emerged.  As a depiction of a highway, traveling between the earth and the sky, and because of its association with seven[lxxv] the pyramid is a material representation of the Elohim.   Those in the Yesod/Daath twilight realm are the Walkers Between Worlds who are empowered by the Elohim and use the geometric function root six to command the Merkabah chariot to travel this road that leads into the heavens, altered states of reality, or other dimensions outside of our own universe.

The adventurer enters the Dark Tree as a single point of light, a star, Lucifer/Sirius, the Morning Star.

It is the union of the point and the circle, the infinitely small and the infinitely large, which create a new universe.

The star is the point of the infinitely small and the circle that of the infinitely large, the future of unknown possibilities.

In this form the practitioner is Sirius the Morning Star, unleashing the inundation of the Nile, the surge of raw cosmic energy containing the rich black substance, the basis of growth.  Egypt

# Howling at the Sky

was known as Khem, the Black Land, because of this black substance brought down by the Nile at the time of the inundation. From Khem came the word alchemy.

The raw primal energy is brought through in this manner to bring life to the Solar Tree.

If the Solar Tree is not balanced, it will be thrown into chaos. The inundation of the Nile river in ancient Egypt brought life to the land. However, it could also be the harbinger of death and destruction if too powerful for the banks of the river and the irrigation systems to handle.

The land of ancient Egypt is an image of man. The inundation is the influx of raw primal energy, bringing life to the land. By becoming an adventurer one can tap infinite reserves of energy for the physical body and one's life. One's world becomes larger and more colorful because of the increase of energy.

"The king and the land are one." This phrase from Arthurian legend means, if the king of the body fails to tap the unlimited reserves of energy beyond Kether or places blocks in consciousness to prevent its flow, then the land becomes barren, symbolizing the loss of the Grail, vitality.

Purity of single mindfulness represented by Sirius[lxxvi] is the discovery of the Grail which renews life. One must be in a prepared state to receive the Grail; otherwise catastrophe results, as illustrated in the above section describing the Nile flood. For the practitioner, the preparation for receiving the rush of life energy is achieved through performing the machines detailed in the chapter Basic Machines.

When Set, the Lord of Upper Egypt and Horus, the Lord of Lower Egypt, are seen together they symbolize the outpouring of raw primal energy from the upper reaches of the Nile, at the time of the inundation, directed through the circuits and channels of Lower Egypt. During the early dynastic periods of Ancient Egypt both Set and Horus were seen as Lords, often represented as a man with two heads, the Horus falcon, and the Set animal. Set and Horus are often depicted together making the symbolic gestures of union of the Two Lands by binding the plants of Upper Egypt, the lotus, and Lower Egypt, the papyrus, around the emblem of union, the divine order, the symbol of the ankh.

It is a representation of adversity and the overcoming of adversity which brings life. The people of this early period realized that both energies, the light and the dark, were required for balanced existence. In the system of the QBL this is demonstrated by the outpour of energy from the dark unknown tree into the known solar tree of the self.

The emergence of new life, which destroys outmoded forms, is often imagined as chaos by those who have not built a structure to handle it. This outpouring of pure energy has no regard for personality that is deficient in the ability to adapt.

Diagram 3-08 illustrates the unicircular hexagram formed from the Golden Section. Note how the Daath Yesod points reach into the outer circles exceeding the boundary of the inner circle. This is the Star of Set who is Lord of the Outside, of the Unknown. It is a symbol of the dynamic principle of growth. It is creative vision into the unknown future, imagination.

Diagram 3-09 depicts the conventional unicursular hexagram where all points fit within the inner circle. It is the Star of Horus, Lord of the Known, and is a protective symbol which maintains the balanced structure of the known, the past.

Diagram 3-09 illustrates the conditions necessary for successfully accessing and integrating the energies represented by diagram 3-08.

Sirius therefore is a union of the past, Horus, and the future, Set. Light and shadow illustrating its twin qualities of the binary star Sirius[lxxvii].

# Howling at the Sky

## The Stars Beyond

The Only Way Out is Through

It is now that the adventurer has arrived at the symbolic crossroads. Here, beneath a dark moon, the pact is made with supernatural, alien forces. In this environment the brave set in motion a sequence of events that will expand the experiences that life can offer them.

The pact is traditionally made with Carfax[lxxviii] who equates with Set, the totem of the unknown future. The faint hearted, who fear the unknown, have perverted this traditional image of opportunity and inverted it to become a jailer, known in the Christian tradition as the Devil. This image has been manufactured as an excuse for not stepping out into the light for fear of being a self empowered and accountable entity. Fear has built their confinement and brought darkness to their world.

The Serpent Path, sometimes referred to as the path of the chameleon, is the sum total of the paths of the QBL Tree of Life. It is through these paths that the practitioner matures over time to become a more genuine vehicle of the life force by acquiring the qualities of a changeling[lxxix]. This quality is an image of the Elohim who are the principle of self creating[lxxx].

What follows is an example of a pathworking to illustrate the dynamics of the technique. From this example readers should be able to develop their own techniques for the other paths making their own inroads into the QBL.

We will be using the path of the Hebrew letter ת that corresponds to the tarot card of the Universe. This path leads from the Sephirah of Malkuth to that of Yesod and is the lowest path on the Tree of Life[lxxxi]. To begin, meditate on the qualities of these two Sephiroth to gain a basic understanding of the energy represented by the path which connects them.  Also, be aware of the overlay patterns of the QBL Tree of Life, (see diagram 1-22), from which it is apparent that there are characteristics of other paths and spheres producing undercurrents adding timbre, depth, and richness to their quality.

Diagram 3-10a illustrates the temple layout for a pathworking of the Hebrew letter ת which corresponds to the Universe card of the tarot.  The outer amber circle is Tiphareth of Assiah and the inner circle, divided into four segments of black, citrine, russet and olive, is the Malkuth of Yetzirah.  The lower circle is a combination of the paths ת of Yetzirah and ג of Assiah.  See diagram 1-22 for an illustration of how these paths combine and resonate with each other.  The upper circle is the union of the Sephiroth Yesod of Yetzirah and Daath of Assiah.  Each of the these segments is colored in its appropriate color correspondence.  Consult  table 2 for color correspondences.  Although it is the path of the Hebrew letter ת of Yetzirah that is being used, the color scales of the corresponding energies of Assiah are incorporated to make you aware of their presence.  It is the intermeshing of the paths and spheres from the various worlds of the Tree of Life of the QBL that bring it to life and cause it to resonate like a musical chord.

Initial banishing machines are performed in the outer circle.  After these have been accomplished, the practitioner moves into the lower circle and performs the machine of Saturn towards the north[lxxxii].  The practitioner then sits in a comfortable posture, relaxes, and travels the tarot card of the Universe.  See diagram 3-10 for an illustration of this card.  After completing the journey the practitioner moves into the upper circle and performs the machine of the Moon to ground the self in the sephiroth of Yesod.  The journey is made from south to north because when the Tree of Life is projected into a sphere, Kether is at the northern pole.

# Howling at the Sky

The image, in the center of the card and dominating it, is Nuit[lxxxiii], the ancient Egyptian goddess of the sky. Her body is sequined with stars and the spheres of Yesod and Daath are also depicted. This was the image on the inside of the sarcophagus lid looking down upon the mummified[lxxxiv] body of the pharaoh[lxxxv]. The veil of four color segments before Nuit corresponds to the colors of Malkuth of Yetzirah, the four elemental aspects of the self your starting point (see table 2). The diagonal lines separating the four colors of Malkuth are the crossroads. Behind Nuit, but presently hidden, are the symbols of Yesod and Daath, the crescent moon for Yesod and the golden section triangle of Sirius for Daath, your destination point (see diagram 3-11).

Prior to working with the card, spend as much time as possible staring and meditating on it so that you can easily visualize it in your imagination.

The working begins by performing the banishing machines of the pentagram and hexagram in the large circle. For initial workings, prior to traveling the path, you may wish to work a sequence of elemental machines, earth, air, water, and fire to build a firm base from which to begin. The elemental tattwa cards, Prithivi, Vayu, Apas and Tejas are ideal vehicles for entering into these regions (see diagram 3-12).

After performing the banishing machines, move into the lower circle, face north, and perform the machine for Saturn. Then light an appropriate incense such as indigo.

Allow several minutes for staring into the card and relaxing. Close your eyes and build the card in your imagination. When the card rises and appears in your imagination, perceive that the image is the lid of a sarcophagus. Continuing to hold the image in your imagination, realize that the illustration is on the inside of the lid and that you lie in the posture of a mummified deceased pharaoh[lxxxvi] within the sarcophagus. The bandages you are wrapped in represent the preserving aspect of earth. For most of us, this has become the rigid body armor that over years of life experience our Ruach[lxxxvii] has manufactured to protect the image we have of ourselves. The granite walls of the sarcophagus represent the limits of the material plane and the images depicted on them are terra-form representations required to enter the dimensions beyond. Meditate on the quality of granite and its relationship to the quality of Saturn, the planetary correspondence of the path. At your feet you see the image of Khepri, the Sun At Night; at your head the image of Mut; on your right side, Nephthys; on your left, Isis. (See diagram 3- 13). Each of these images is a door of opportunity that opens into the elemental regions they represent.

You now begin to move upward and into the star-studded body of Nuit, finding yourself immersed in a myriad of stars. Continuing to move forward, the stars are all around you, brilliant iridescent bubbles in an infinite ocean of indigo. As you meditate on and bathe in the stars, you discern that some are more prominent than others. You find your self drawn to these specific stars. Upon arriving at them, you discover you can penetrate and travel into them. What you encounter in them are previous experiences from your life, unresolved experiences and encounters. They are time capsules enabling you to time travel and see how you interacted with the adventure you were offered in those previous periods of your life. Your initial journeys should be devoted to these experiments. This will help relieve suppressed and unresolved issues in your life.

After several experiments, you will begin to detect a consistent thread or theme in experiencing these memories. The feeling is akin to the undefined fear one sometimes experiences when walking in the dark. You sense that something is present but cannot rationally explain it. Grotesque images and experiences,

# Howling at the Sky

and a sense of dread and anxiety will quite often begin to surface. When these feeling and images occur, it is an indication that you are making progress, for you are accessing the suppressed energies of your subconscious. You are facing the truth about yourself, contrary to the image your Ruach has built for itself. This is an irrational fear, built up over years, that has secretly prevented you from achieving your full potential. The reaction of the Ruach to this emerging energy is to manifest the Lurker at the Threshold of Lord Bulwer Lytton's book, *Zanoni*. What is occurring is the Ruach, the reasoning mind, sees the image of itself being threatened by the release of these energies, exposing to consciousness the true condition of what you are, which is not the image that the Ruach has created for itself. The Ruach, over years, has been given license to usurp its position by identifying itself as the be all and end all of what you are, the inflated ego. This is important to note: images that manifest fear are important because they can bring growth when you confront and overcome them. Images that manifest comfort encourage inertia and weakness.

As you continue to travel and experience more and more life experiences, they open up like a flood of refreshing water to a parched and arid land.

After several experiences, you begin to feel a sense of calm and the body of stars merge to coagulate around you to form the Egyptian frog[lxxxviii] headed goddess, Heket. You now terra-form[lxxxix] into the body of Heket and arrive in the sphere of Yesod. Successful arrival and simulation with Yesod and Heket will empower you with the ability of a voltigeur[xc]. The ability of the frog to leap is used as a symbol of leaping the Abyss, a quality of Daath, the sephirah underlying Yesod.

As you gaze down on the path you have traveled, you discover that the stars in the body of Nuit are frogspawn birthed by the terra-form you are assuming, Heket. Realize your life experiences have been given birth by you and reinforce the concept that you are accountable and responsible for your life experiences and actions. This is the act of sacrifice, the giving up of the false image one has of one's old self to become light enough to escape the gravity of ת and Malkuth.

If this realization and sacrifice does not occur, the traveler falls through Yesod of Yetzirah into the Daath of Assiah.

When this occurs, the self will be perceived as a falling star tumbling through space[xci] destined to become another star, life experience, in the body of Nuit. Upon closer examination, you will realize that the trail behind you forms a tail and you have terra-formed into the aspect of a human sperm. In this guise, you penetrate the sphere of Assiah at the sphere of Daath, impregnating the High Priestess, the tarot card that corresponds with the path ג, with the lessons learned from the journey.

Within the incubating body of the High Priestess you descend into the sphere of Tiphareth, your starting point and unite with the High Priest and become the Shekinah[xcii] of Malkuth of Yetzirah[xciii]. This may occur several times[xciv] before successful terra-form of Heket and establishment in Yesod is achieved. However, each time you return you will bring knowledge[xcv] that can be assimilated to be used for future experiences that will culminate in successful Heket terra-form.

By returning as the Light Bringer, you manifest, because of casting a shadow, the blocks that imprison you, the Achons. In realizing your imprisonment, you are offered the opportunity of escape.

If these experiences take place on a sub-conscious level, as sometimes occurs, then individuals may believe they are having intercourse with extraterrestrial intelligence, usually characterized as alien abduction or intrusion[xcvi]. If there is a strong alienation between the inner self and the reasoning mind,

## Howling at the Sky

it is possible the returning inner self may be experienced as an hallucination of an alien spacecraft. Encounters with gods, angels, succubus, incubus and faery realm abductions may also fall into this class of experience[xcvii]. Throughout human history there have been a multitude of recorded experiences that fall into this category.

This is not to deny an individual's encounter with alien intelligence from other planets may not have occurred or is occurring. However, I am inclined to believe that these encounters, if of extraterrestrial origin, are occurring on astral realms. What ever they are, they experience us more often than not on a mental rather than physical level. From the above example it should be possible for each practitioner to now develop their own pathways into the lost domain of themselves, the mirror of all that is.

These experiences will culminate in the acquisition of your lost innocence, the Fool of the tarot allocated to a the first letter of the Hebrew alphabet.

# Roger Williamson

# Howling at the Sky

## Soul Catcher

The Opening of the gates of the infinite and the powering of the Merkabah vehicle.

The machine that follows will inevitably have dramatic repercussions for the practitioner conditioned into believing in the demonic qualities of the inverted pentagram. A practitioner with a one-sided, rigid worldview is liable to violently shatter his/her universe with devastating results by using this machine. The individual programmed into this specific mindset should spend much time in meditating on what opposes his/her point of view before performing the following machine.

Because of the antagonism the inverted pentagram symbol arouses I will explain the two modes of the figure. It should be noted however, that the pentagram, whether inverted or not, contains its opposite in its midst. The pentagram with a single point at the top, (diagram 3-14) contains in its center the inverted pentagram and the inverted pentagram with two points at the top contains in its center the pentagram with a single point at the top. This illustrates how everything contains its opposite.

The pentagram with a single point at the top, (diagram 3-14) is the image of how we see ourselves. For this reason it is a symbol of protection. It places us in the world with which we are familiar. It is also the higher aspects of the self suppressing the four elemental aspects of ourselves.

The pentagram with one point directed vertically down, (diagram 3-15) often imagined as a symbol of evil, is the sign of the adventurer, the individual who is involved in life. This is the mark of Cain and the symbol of Set. It is the individual delving into the subconscious underworld to find the reality of the true self, rather than being content with the present image of the self, symbolized a pentagram with one point at the top. It is the gate to the underworld. This symbol is often imagined as evil by those who wish to escape the reality of life because of the adversity and challenge it evokes. It is the head of the goat Capricorn, adversity, challenge, and the mountains we must climb to be alive. The Sun is at its lowest point when in the sign of Capricorn. This is the period of winter when the nights are longer than the days. Capricorn on the Tree of Life is the path of the Hebrew letter ע meaning eye, which is allocated to the Devil card of the tarot. With this eye we open up and bring light to the unknown adventure land as seen by the daring individual as a life that is a sequence of problem solving events. The solving of one problem entitles the initiate to progress to the next more complicated and challenging problem. With this attitude we realize that life is the moment and act with the noblest of our abilities to do the best we can with each moment offered to us.

The machine of the Overture harmonizes the practitioner's self to the macrocosm. It represents the magician finding his/her place in the universe and being there, symbolized by becoming aware of the hidden axis at the core of all that exists. Once this state is achieved the practitioner is ready to begin receiving the messages that will inform him/her on how to build the Merkabah.

The Rite of Set moves the practitioner into the worlds outside of the universe by using the vehicle of the Merkabah. By inscribing the inverted pentagrams between the quarters he/she opens up the gates of the between worlds, the paths of the Tree of Life, the dynamic powers of transformation. These can be summed up in the energy zone of Daath, the relationship between the three Supernals of Kether, Chokmah and Binah, represented by the god Set. It is the twilight realm.

This is the sacrificial part of the rite, the investing of your achievements and ideas of self into the future. It is realizing that

# Howling at the Sky

all of your achievements were only on loan, and that they are the currency that will purchase your ticket into new areas of encounter. What you realize in this act of sacrifice is neither you nor your achievements are very important in the great plan, what is important is experience and expression of self in right action. Daath is the origin of form and yet is without form because it is a function.

The final act of the machine, the reciting of the summons, constructs the vehicle of the Merkabah.

The practitioner who has diligently practiced the techniques given so far should not need to use my following summons. It is given as an example only. The key is, by using the techniques given previously, you can assemble your own symbol and reference system to translate the messages from the void. There will be similarities because the laws of geometry are universal. What will differ will be your interpretation of how those laws apply to your situation and life circumstances.

In diagram 3-16a is illustrated the center piece of the temple layout for the Rite of Set. The design is a representation of the symbolic cross roads, the place in magical tradition where the soul makes its pact with supernatural forces. The diagonal lines are the geometric functions that are the vehicle of transcendence, the lines of communication into the adventure zone. There are twelve visible double cubes that emphasize wholeness, a cycle, the condition we desire to overcome. The center square is the base of the thirteenth double cube that launches the practitioner into the adventure zone of new and original life situations. In the north of the circle is the number eleven representing the penetration of the veil of Isis. Further to the north beyond the circle should be visualized the Energy terra-form of Taweret. In the south is seventy five, the number of Lucifer symbolic of the practitioner awakening to new life situations.

Diagram 3-16a can also be used as an astral gateway by utilizing the same technique as practiced with the tattwa and tarot cards and as a base for mounting a crystal ball when scrying.

An explanation of the symbolism of the text is given at the end of the rite.

# Howling at the Sky

## Angels with Burning Wings Have Knowledge of Fire: The Rite of Set

No altar is used in this machine because diagram 3-16a is placed in the center of the circle. The four elemental weapons, instead of being arranged on the altar, are placed at their respective cardinal points on the circumference of the circle: fire wand in the south, water cup in the west, air dagger in the east, and the pentacle in the north .

Seven green candles are placed outside of the circle and four candles, in their appropriate elemental colors, are placed at the cardinal quarters (see diagram 3-16). If you cannot use candles, try using stones of an appropriate color instead.

A tripod is positioned in the center of the circle surmounted by the Machine diagram. This diagram should ideally be at the eye level of the magician (see diagram 2-01).

Begin by performing the machine of the Overture. At the end of each elemental evoking section of this machine place the appropriate elemental weapon in the center of the circle. This is a symbolic gesture of taking all that you are and investing it in the vacuum of the future. It is the act of sacrifice. The future is a vacuum because it is as yet devoid of life.

Next light the incense and bring from the outside of the circle the seven candles, arranging them within the circle to match the configuration of the constellation of the Great Bear, (see diagram 3-17). Go to the northeast of the circle and face that direction. With your left hand inscribe an inverted pentagram while vibrating Daath. Move counter-clockwise around the circle, inscribing the inverted pentagram and vibrating Daath between each of the quarters while spiraling toward the center of the circle. Northwest, southwest, southeast, and finish by standing on the center of the circle. Now go to the south, face north, and repeat the following summons:

*1. By the number eleven and by the inverted five pointed star, head of the goat god lord Set I summon thee.*

*2. Set, lord of the desert waste, lord of storms, lord of change, lord of the outside I summon thee.*

*3. Hear me for I am Anubis, Opener of the Way, he of the jackal head, howler in the waste.*

*4. I eat the fruit of the sacred garden and exile myself from safety partaking in the Dark Rite.*

*5. By the action of the diagonal I summon you Lord Set to open the gate of Daath, that the waters of Nu may flood this circle.*

*6. Ascend! Reveal yourself intractable thrust of life from the swelling depths of brooding possibility.*

*7. Come original future realms and speak to me in your vibrant language of transforming principle.*

*By the number eleven and by the inverted five pointed star, head of the goat god Lord Set I summon thee.*

*8. I see the circles of the two worlds, symbol of the infinite, eclipse and from their center see that which was hidden revealed.*
*9. Vesica gate unfold and open, as did the lotus on the waters of Nu at the beginning of time.*
*10. Oh delicate flower of transient shining glory plunge your thirsting roots into the rich velvet pool of night.*

# Howling at the Sky

*11. Be the vehicle of my dissident spirit that I may peel off my past to traverse the miraculous spiral of opening.*
*12. That I may live for the moment within the adventure land of boundless stars of opportunity.*
*13. The celebration of you Lord Set is the Golden Section, harmonious creation that unfolds into the unknown future.*

*By the number eleven and by the inverted five pointed star, head of the goat god Lord Set I summon thee.*

*14. Lord Set I have opened the dimension gate in the desert of your realm and the highway to the stars is before me.*
*15. I take the gate and walk between worlds to partake in the Dark Rite, the Eternal Return, to drink the waters of Nu.*
*16. I unite with thee Sun behind the Sun, in this sacred place that I have constructed in your honor.*
*17. That the ghost songs of my ancestors may echo through my being in symphonies of cathedral proportion.*
*18. By the code of my birth right I mutate with cavalier abandon into a spirit with burnished wings.*
*19. My number is eleven and I stand between the four and nine.*

*By the number eleven and by the inverted five pointed star, head of the goat god Lord Set I welcome thee.*

Move to the center of the circle and sit within legs of the tripod. Using diagram 1-19, project into the plane. After completing your vision record the results and then clear the area with the Banishing Machines of the Hexagram and Pentagram.

Commentary

# Roger Williamson

1. Eleven is the number of Daath, the transforming principle. The inverted five pointed star is the entrance into unknown territory. You are stating you wish to transform yourself to deal with new life situations or to experience altered states of reality. In summoning Set, totem of the outside, you are declaring you wish to experience and acquire knowledge of what is presently unknown, original or untapped states of consciousness. It is repeated through the summons to insure that the mind remains focused on the object of the rite.

2. These attributes of Set will become the character of the practitioner, at the height of the machine, as observed by one who has not attained this degree of experience.

3. The practitioner assumes the energy terra-form of Anubis. Anubis is the Pole Star, who at the beginning of any endeavor, is the focal point that opens the universe from out of the void of space by uttering the first word, a howl, the origin of speech. Anubis calls on the dynamic principle of Set to take the universe out of wholeness that it may transform. This call is answered by the rising of the star Sirius.

4. The fruit of the sacred garden is the forbidden fruit of Eden which bestows knowledge. Meaning the fruit falls from the Tree of Life to enter and experience a new dimension. The practitioner acknowledges by this statement that he/she has reached a state of wholeness, the body of the mother, which desires to be transformed. The declaration of technique is then proclaimed, which is the Dark Rite. The Dark Rite is symbolic of the black silt brought down the Nile by the inundation of that river. The ancient name of Egypt is Khem, meaning "black land" from which came the word alchemy. Alchemy is the transmutation of a base substance into its higher aspect, represented in the Nile valley by the transmutation of the black silt becoming rich vegetation. The Dark Rite is the action of acquiring knowledge of what was

# Howling at the Sky

unknown, symbolically represented by the black silt brought down by the Nile from the unknown regions of its source in the South. This may seem a contradiction to the north being the source of all. However, the north is the source of all, the Mother, but she is manifested out of the south by her son Set, represented by the star Sirius. Note the appearance of opposites, north and south, the bright star Sirius, and the black silt of life.

5. The diagonal is the root six function which is the action of Set. It is the 1=10 Golden Dawn earth grade sign which cracks open the known universe of the practitioner. The waters of Nu are the raw influx of original action and thought entering into the practitioners opened sphere. When the practitioner opens Daath of Yetzirah an opening is made into Yesod of Briah (see diagram 1-22). The waters of Nu, the path ה of Briah, then travel from Briah into Yetzirah refreshing the mind with inspiration that can be actualized in Assiah. Refer to chapter The Stars Beyond for an analysis of the this action on the planes of Yetzirah and Assiah.

6. The action of transformation is symbolically announced by the ascension of the star Sirius. This proceeds the manifestation of black residue from the source of the Nile which is the vehicle of originality.

7. The practitioner accepts that life is change.

8. The circles of the worlds are the infinite past and the infinite future. That which is revealed is cognizance that life is the moment. This is the engaging of the gears of the machine, the gears being the worlds of the QBL.

9. Vesica Gate, the sphere of Yesod of Briah and Daath of Yetzirah. The waters of Nu symbolically represent the inundation of the Nile river.

10. Wholeness fathoms the depths for the source of all.

11. The sacrifice of what one has achieved for further experience in an unfolding universe.

12. We accept that life is change.
13. The turning on of the Merkabah.
14. The gate is open and the infinite possibility of the future awaits.
15. The commitment to be more than you are whatever the consequences.
16. The practitioner becomes one with Sirius the star of Set, the eight within the seven, the acquiring of gnosis.
17. The bloodline of the practitioner is contacted and speaks to power the Merkabah.
18. The birthright is that you can be anything you want to be, you can be more than you are. This is the power of the Merkabah.
19. My number is eleven and I stand between the four and nine. The fourth path is the

Empress, the ninth path is Strength, and between them is the Sephirah Daath. Four plus nine equals thirteen, which is אחד the Hebrew word for unity and unity equals wholeness. This is saying that Daath is the seed within unity which will transform it.

The fourth path means door, the ninth path means serpent so wholeness, thirteen, is the door of the serpent. The Garden of Eden was a state of wholeness, an image of the Mother, that had become complacent because of perfectly balanced opposites, requiring the entrance of the serpent to transform it. The serpent was the disrupter of perfect balance and was the guide to the seed, Daath, which was contained within the fruit that was a microcosmic image of the whole garden. The seed is the hidden potential, the child of the future and the quality of that future will depend on how we react to the original life situations presented to us.

As has been said, wholeness must transform if it is to continue to be a vehicle of life. The serpent is generally depicted as evil because it threatens what we have achieved. It puts us into life-

# Howling at the Sky

challenging situations which require us to work. Human nature generally seeks achievement so that it can sit back. This is contrary to what life demands from the gift it has given us.
The angel preventing Adam and Eve returning to the garden symbolizes that once we have taken a step we cannot go back. We cannot change the past but we can learn from the past to impact upon the future.
The midpoint between 4 and 9 is 6.5. 6.5 x 10=65, the number of אדני conscious dimension interface and LVX gnosis. 6 + 5=11 that is Daath, the revealer of the Sephiroth above the Abyss and the god Set.
Eleven is attributed to the tarot card of Justice, Hebrew letter ל, that connects the Sephirah of Tiphareth value six and Geburah value five.
20. The practitioner terra-forms into Set, the totem of the geometric function of Daath, the gears of the machine are engaged and the Merkabah is powered.

For two practitioners
The sorcerer, who is the controller of the ceremony, assumes the form of a jackal to represent the Opener of the Way, Anubis.
The medium, who is the channel, sits in the middle of the of circle within the tripod legs on top of diagram 3-16, the base of the thirteenth double cube that is the gate of the adventure zone. Facing south he/she assumes the energy terra-form of Set. The medium represents the point of light entering the Dark Tree to trigger the inundation of pure primal energy.
Each participant should wear a purple or black robe with a lamen symbolic of Sirius around the neck suspended from a purple ribbon.
Faces and hands should be painted purple and streaked with yellow. Position eleven purple candles equally spaced apart

around the circle.

Open the temple using the Overture Machine to establish the balance of the Solar Tree. This symbolizes the land organized and ready to receive and channel the inundation of raw primal energy. After completion of the Overture light the incense (a mixture of dittany of crete and oppopanax works well).

If circumstances allow, include a fire within the circle. If you are working in an enclosed environment, use a candle to avoid asphyxiation.

The inverted pentagrams are now inscribed with the left hand between the quarters in an anti-clockwise direction to open the gate of Daath, the highway between worlds, the regions between the north, south, east, and west. After inscribing each of the pentagrams, vibrate Daath.

The summons is then recited standing in the south facing north to energize the Merkabah chariot.

While reciting the summons let the conjurer observe a vortex of energy forming around the inside rim of the circle. The image of the vortex should be of a galaxy, a great wheel of spiraling primal energy. Let this vortex grow in strength moving in an counter-clockwise motion around the circle. Increasing in power let the vortex expand inward and center on the medium seated upon the sigil.

Feel the tremendous concentration of energy building around the medium. When the concentration of energy reaches its peak, let it explode upward in a spiraling column of energy. Let the column become the god-form of Set towering above and around the medium. Now is the medium ready to transmit the function and word of Set.

Ingress to the Set Plane

# Howling at the Sky

The medium sits facing north in the center of the circle within the legs of the tripod. The medium then visualizes an Egyptian portal in dull red sandstone. Above the portal the medium should see the vulture goddess Nekhbet in shades of green. Within the gate opening see the Lucifer/ Sirius sigil, (diagram 1-19) and project yourself through it. After passing through the gate you will observe a pyramid which is produced from the Golden Section. This pyramid you approach at a corner so that two sides are visible, the right side being slightly larger (see diagram 3-02).

You will observe that the apex of the pyramid is twisted at an angle to the left. Twist yourself to the left so that the pyramid is vertical.

You have now aligned yourself to the plane by altering your sense of perspective. This twist of consciousness gives the ability to travel from one plane of reality to another. This ability can be practiced by looking at the hexagon, (diagram 1-15) and drawing out the cube from its body.

After several performances of the rite to gain some experience in achieving inner plane contact, I recommend that the medium use the ring and disc[xcviii], pendulum or ouija board to acquire answers to questions asked by the conjurer. With this technique there is less chance of ego contamination because answers to questions are revealed through numerical and geometric codes, the language of the infinite.

In tapping primal energy you manifest your hidden suppressed potential. The power that is your birthright. However, be aware of what has been said about balancing the Solar Tree before initiating the inundation of raw primal energy into your sphere of awareness.

# Roger Williamson

# Howling at the Sky

## The Howling

Nothing prepares you for Cairo.  You can read books, watch documentaries, listen to other peoples accounts of arriving at this gateway city between east and west but nothing prepares you for the mayhem and sense of chaos.  Five days ago I arrived in this sprawling shambled metropolis and I continue to feel very disorientated.  My mind seems to have taken on the personality of the rambling serpentine coils of this city. I feel out of control as situations present themselves and I stumble like a drunken man trying to fathom the meanings of the mundane.  They just have a different way of doing things here which is definitely contrary to a western mind.  We are so used to clearly defined arrangements, but, here everything is flexible and adaptable to change.  Every question about the days plans is replied to by "no problem", meaning we will take care of it.  After several days you realize amazingly, that they do.

Peace, there is no peace.  Every minute of every day your senses are bombard by an exotic cacophony of  alien language, smells and visions that are superimposed upon wailing electronic rhythms of contemporary middle eastern melodies.  Then, quite suddenly, from out of this seeming pandemonium you hear one of the five haunting calls to prayer that spirals up to marry the confusion into a rich and mysterious mandala.

This collage of overwhelming sensory impressions is carried upon the heaving serpent of pollution that writhes through the zigzagging alleys and streets with scales of spangled dust.  Methodically and incessantly this serpent wends its way while shedding its scales of contamination leaving nothing immune from its caress .

If Cairo sleeps, its between three and five am.  However, this is only true from Monday through Friday, for, weekends have no distinction between night and day. The streets are equally packed with party revelry what ever the hour. In contradiction to the west, the inhabitants here are more concerned with interacting with each other rather than with the solitary accumulation of material possessions

It was from within this glorious mayhem that at eight am one morning I took a taxi to the stepped pyramid of Sakkarah arriving at its remote location about an hour later. The site lies just outside of the fertile area of the Nile valley, south west of Cairo. Not bothering to wait for me to get out my driver sank himself down in the drivers seat, put a newspaper over his head to shield his eyes from the sun, and told me he would wait for my return.

I emerged onto the lunar like landscape and was immediately griped by the peace and sense of solitude. After the chaos of Cairo, it was reminiscent of having a cooling balm massaged onto a fiery insect bit. The peace washed over and refreshed me in a rhythm of euphoric waves. I don't think I have ever experienced a quietness quite like it. I was sure that I could literally hear a pin drop from yards away.

The desert wasn't as I had imagined it. I expected sand, but found it was actually composed of boulders, shale and pieces of rock fragments. I bent down and let my hand stroke across the surface and picked up a thin veneer of white dust across my palm and fingers.

I walked towards the reconstructed entrance at the southwest corner of the complex and observed, even at this early hour, tourists approaching up the road from the valley. Amazingly not even our presence disturbed the peace and rejuvenating qualities of the site. It was as though we were separate, insulated from the site by some invisible sphere. It was as though the timeless guardians of this necropolis shielded themselves from the contamination of modern man by creating force fields around the

# Howling at the Sky

intruders. Like a holographic images, we moved through the tumbled stones and left as much of an impact as light passing across the surface of a lake.

Running the gauntlet between the locals and paying the traditional bakshish, I entered into the shade of a shallow vestibule which had an opening on the far wall that led into the court of the complex. On the right hand wall of this vestibule engraved in the limestone was a false door. The detail of this door was so accurate and precise, that it even included the hinge pins and sockets. I remembered reading somewhere that it was through this false door that the pharaoh's ka would pass unimpeded as he traveled this funeral complex that was the replica of his kingdom. I shifted my attention to the left hand wall and was confronted by another engraving. This was of two figures pouring what appeared to be water over each other. On closer scrutiny, I discerned that it was not water but ankhs, the timeless symbol of life. I began to walk on but was suddenly stopped in my tracks by memory. I returned to the image of the two figures. I realized that I knew them. These ancient stone etchings possessed the physical characteristics and features of the woman who marked the arrival of the machine and the man of the ritual. Surly it couldn't be. The resemblance was startling. I reached out my hand and let it follow the lines of the engravings. As I did so, my mind recalled the experiences of those so long ago adventures; and, in the curves of the etchings, I was bestowed a sense of arrival. I stood back contemplating the scene, absorbing its essence. I wanted to be able to recall it as accurately as possible so I could take relief from its essence long after my visit. A wave of tourists suddenly entered and passed by, bringing me out of my reverie. I took a final look at the wall and passed on. Walking further, I entered a colonnade of pillars carved in the image of palm stems, and after passing through these, I emerged into the great south court. Here I found myself confronted by a section of reconstructed wall bearing a frieze of cobras, symbolic of the goddess Wadjet.

I looked right and saw across the vast courtyard the beginnings of architecture, the stark stepped pyramid of Zoser, designed and built by the architect Imhotep. I contemplated on what might have been the origins of this man who was later made into a demi god by the people of Egypt. What power of imagination this man must have possessed. I say man, although we don't know for sure if he was a man or a woman. What were the origins of this individual's imagination. Maybe it wasn't imagination; maybe, it was knowledge already possessed, brought with him from another place to bequeath to the inhabitants of this region. If he did bring it with him, then from where, if this is the first known stone building erected on Earth.

A group of European looking tourists came from behind me jabbering in a language that I didn't recognize and passing by me headed out across the courtyard in the direction of the pyramid. I decided to wait a while and allow them to get a reasonable distance ahead of me before heading in the same direction. While waiting I walked west and came to a pit that I knew from the guide book to be Zoser's southern burial chamber. As pharaoh of both upper and lower Egypt, it was required for political etiquette that he be symbolically buried in both kingdoms. The opening of the pit was fenced in, for obvious reasons, but, where I stood, there was a gate and beyond it a flight of descending stone steps. Looking beyond the gate at the first step, I was taken aback to see the image of a bat traced in the dust. My mind was driven back through the vortex of time, now seeming so long ago, to when I found the dead bat nailed to a gate post on the occasion of my discovering the machine. I urgently looked around, feeling someone had approached me but

# Howling at the Sky

found myself still alone. My consciousness heightened. I took time to take in the details of the entrance of the pit. Suddenly I saw that it had the proportions of a double square. I heard the opening of the pit howl upward at the sky, speaking in a language of unimaginable age. It was a tumultuous howling of draconian arcane speech. Here I knew, was the gate to Amenti, the underworld. In the long annuls of human history, heroes like Orpheus and Dante had stood at such sites contemplating the opportunity they had been offered, questioning the strength of their resolve to enter into the adventure zone. At this moment I pushed open the gate and placed my right foot on the first descending step erasing the image of the bat. As I did so, the heroes of history stood alongside me and I joined them in their timeless fellowship.

# Roger Williamson

# Howling at the Sky

# Part IV

# Roger Williamson

# Howling at the Sky

# Machines

A machine is a system that converts energy from one form into another: it is a vehicle of transformation. Machines can be used to transport people or things from one place to another, communicate with other life forms, and shape or transmute materials.

Magic is a machine that is used to transport you from one place to another, communicate with other life forms, shape and transmute you.

The following machines are to be committed to memory. I recommend that initially a minimum of one month be dedicated to each machine for memorization. Once memorized, a machine need only be performed periodically to maintain proficiency.

The banishing machines are performed to balance and align yourself to your true place in the universe. The invoking machines are performed to receive the individual pieces of the message for constructing the Merkabah chariot. The banishing and invoking machines build the circuits required to channel the energy of the messages being received. If these messages are received, without the channels being fully in place, then catastrophe occurs for the practitioner. You will either become a creature devoid of will or a raging fanatic who believes their way is the only way. This can be symbolized by the inundation of the Nile overflowing its banks; because of lack of preparation, it destroys the structured order of the land.

The machines that follow are readily available in numerous books on ceremonial magic but are included to give coherency and flow to the methods being explained.

# Roger Williamson

# Howling at the Sky

## Banishing Machines

## The Banishing Machine Of The Pentagram

The realigning of the self

The banishing machine of the pentagram is used to realign ourselves. During the course of the day we are bombarded with many situations which result in the various aspects of ourselves falling out of alignment. This first machine is used to correct this misalignment and create a firm base from which we may reach for the stars.

The machine begins and ends with the QBL Cross, which is a symbolic representation of the geometric function root two. This is the basis of all ceremonial magic, which is the accomplishing of synthesis through dynamic change. The QBL cross is a transforming principle because the diagonals of the root two function transform the rigidity of the square, a symbol of the self, the microcosm, into a three dimensional tetrahedron of fire. Diagram1-16: you are required to make a shift in perspective to see this three sided pyramid of fire.

From this cross emerges another larger square, the side of which is equal to the diagonal of the square of the self from which it emerged (see diagram 4-01).

This square is created by the magician inscribing the pentagrams and evoking the Archangels at the four quarters. The second larger square is symbolic of the macrocosm, the elemental world outside of the self. The formula can be summed up by the expression "As above so below."

At the close of the machine wholeness is again divided by repeating the QBL cross, symbolizing that all is change.

The performance of the QBL Cross at the beginning of the machine states what it is you wish to achieve through the performance of the machine. It is repeated at the close of the machine to show that you have accomplished what you set out to do, which was symbolized by the first QBL Cross.

This is standard for all machines. First, state your intent for the machine. Next, evoke or invoke the energies by use of the machine and finally, seal the machine with the symbol of your accomplishment that was first announced at the beginning.

An appropriate energy terra-form to assume for this machine is the ancient Egyptian jackal-headed god Anubis, eater of the dead. In the wild the jackal is a scavenger, a being that through the process of digestion takes a dead[xcix] thing and turns it into life, by assimilating it into its own body. In the banishing machine of the pentagram we are doing just this. We are re-assimilating the parts of ourselves or aspects of our lives which have become unbalanced, dead things which if not recycled breed disease, and digesting them back into ourselves. We feed on ourselves and our actions so that we can come to know who we are and refine ourselves. This process is sometimes referred to as alchemy. In the ancient Egyptian Book of the Dead this procedure is depicted by the scale section in the Judgment Scene[c].

Begin by facing east and spend a few minutes relaxing yourself. When relaxed, visualize a sphere of brilliant white light above your head. With the index finger of your right hand touch this sphere and then lower your hand to your forehead, drawing down a column of the white light. Perform the following.

Touch forehead and vibrate *ATOH* (thou art)
Touch breast and vibrate *MALKUTH* (the kingdom)
Touch right shoulder and vibrate *VE-GEBURAH* (and the power)
Touch left shoulder and vibrate *VE-GEDULAH* (and the glory)
Clasp hands before self and vibrate *LE-OLAM*

(for ever)

Vibrate *AMEN*[ci]

With the index finger of your right hand inscribe in the east before you the banishing pentagram and vibrate the divine name *IHVH*. Visualize the pentagram in brilliant blue (see diagram 4-02).

With your arm outstretched move to the south.

Keep your arm outstretched between each of the quarters to create a white ring of fire between the pentagrams.

Inscribe pentagram and vibrate *ADONAI*. Move to the west.

Inscribe pentagram and vibrate *EHEIEH*. Move to the north.

Inscribe pentagram and vibrate *AGLA*. Move to the east and complete the circle.

The pentagrams are visualized as blazing blue in color and the circle between them in white.

Stand with arms outstretched as a cross facing east and say:

"Before me Raphael, behind me Gabriel, at my right hand Michael, at my left hand Auriel."

See the archangels in their elemental colors and surroundings. To aid visualization, the Archangels are seen as human but really they are the forces of nature that are neither human nor superhuman.

Say. *"For around me flame the pentagrams and within me shines the six-rayed star."*

Repeat the QBL cross.

The divine names and those of the Archangels are formula for differing aspects of energy.

## The Banishing Machine of the Hexagram
### The realigning of the self to the macrocosm

This machine requires that you assume certain postures. For illustrations of these postures, see diagram 4-03. Descriptions are given below. While making the these signs also assume the corresponding Egyptian terra-form of the energy involved (see diagram 3-13).

Osiris Slain: stand up straight, feet together, arms stretched out horizontally forming a cross.

Mourning of Isis: right arm stretched out horizontally bent at elbow forearm raised vertical. Left arm stretched out horizontally, bent at the elbow with forearm pointing downward.

Apophis and Typhon: arms raised up at 45 degrees forming a V shape.

Osiris Slain and Risen: arms crossed over the breast forming a cross.

This machine is in three parts. Part A the analysis of the Key Word, Part B the inscribing of the figures and Part C is a repeat of the analysis of the Key Word.

Part A

Analysis of the Key Word I.N.R.I

Face east while making the Sign of Osiris Slain and say,

*I. N. R. I. Yod Nun Resh Yod*

Yod Nun Resh Yod is the Hebrew translation of I.N.R.I.

*Virgo, Isis Mighty Mother*

Speak softly. The tone and level of your voice should be representative of the energy with which you are working. Represents the Garden of Eden before the fall. Wholeness that has become stagnant. The Sephirah Netzach on the Tree of Life.

*Scorpio Apophis Destroyer*

Speak loudly. Represents the Serpent in Eden, the power of the path נ on the Tree of Life.

*Sol Osiris Slain and Risen*

Speak in a tone between that of Isis and Apophis. Steady and

# Howling at the Sky

authoritatively. Represents the Garden of Eden after the fall, which symbolizes consciousness and being aware of circumstances. The vehicle has transformed and moved successfully into a new state of reality, the Sephiroth Tiphareth on the Tree of Life.

A successful transition has been made from the elemental realm of the four lower Sephira, the microcosm into the greater world of the macrocosm, the six remaining Sephira.

*Isis, Apophis, Osiris*

*I. A. O.* The light of gnosis achieved through traversing of the path of ג on the QBL Tree of Life.

*The Sign of Osiris Slain.* Speak in a monotone. Make Sign.
*The Sign of the Mourning of Isis.* Speak softly. Make Sign.
*The Sign of Apophis and Typhon.* Speak loudly. Make Sign.
*The Sign of Osiris Risen.* Speak in a steady commanding tone. Make Sign.
*L.* Make Sign.
*V.* Make Sign.
*X.* Make Sign.
*Lux light, the light of the cross.* Make Sign.


Part B
See diagram 4-04 for the four forms of the hexagram used in this machine.
The word ARARITA vibrated at each quarter is an anagram for "one is his beginning one is his individuality his permutation is one."
    Assume the energy terra-form of Horus for this section.

Horus as light manifests the shadows of the blocks that impede our progress.

Before you in the east inscribe the banishing hexagram of fire in red and vibrate *ARARITA*.
Go to the south and inscribe the banishing hexagram of earth in indigo and vibrate *ARARITA*.
Go to the west and inscribe the banishing hexagram of air in yellow and vibrate *ARARITA*.
Go to the north and inscribe the banishing hexagram of water in blue and vibrate *ARARITA*.
Note that for machines of the hexagram the allocation of the elements is accorded to their placement in the zodiac.

Part C
Repeat analysis of the Key Word I.N.R.I. (see section A).

# Howling at the Sky

## Invoking Machines

Once you have balanced and aligned yourself to the universe, you may begin building your receiver for translating the messages from the void. The composite of the messages will be the blueprint of the Merkabah chariot which is your vehicle of attainment.

Each of the invoking machines which follow give a piece of the total message.

## The Greater Machine Of The Pentagram
Awakening the abodes of the elements

See diagram 4-05 for illustrations of the different forms of the pentagram used in this machine.

As in the machine of the Hexagram this machine also requires that you assume certain postures. For illustrations of these postures, see diagram 4-03b.

Earth sign, make forward step with left foot, raise right arm at forty five degrees pointing forward and upward, left arm at forty five degrees downward and backward. Attributed to Malkuth.

Water sign, feet together and hands form water symbol of stomach. Attributed to Hod.

Air sign, feet together, palms face upward as though supporting pillars. Attributed to Yesod.

Fire sign, feet together, hands form fire symbol at forehead. Attributed to Netzach.

Portal sign, feet together, hands at chest gripping imaginary curtains. You then make a symbolic gesture of opening curtains by moving hands outward so the you stand in the image of a cross. It is symbolic of moving beyond the material universe of the elements into the dimension of spirit.

It is traditional to use elemental weapons for these machines. A dagger with a yellow painted handle and hilt for air; a blue cup or clear glass for water; a round disc of wood or clay painted in the colors of Malkuth of Briah (see table 2) for earth; a fire wand made from a 12" long round piece of iron painted red for fire. See *The Golden Dawn* by Israel Regardie, [Llewellyn Publications, 1986] for illustrations and descriptions of traditional ceremonial elemental weapons and consecration ceremonies for them.

Begin as always by performing banishing machines and then move to the quarter corresponding to the element you intend to work with. If you are bringing the elements to you as in evocations: Earth - north, Air - east, Water - west and Fire - south. If you are traveling to a specific elemental plane: Earth - south, Air - west, Water - north and Fire - east.

Face the appropriate elemental quarter and inscribe in white the spirit pentagram before you while vibrating the associated names (see diagram 4-05: passive for earth and water, active for air and fire).

For earth vibrate *NANTA* while inscribing the pentagram and *AGLA* while inscribing the spirit figure.

For water vibrate *HCOMA* while inscribing the pentagram and *AGLA* while inscribing the spirit figure.

For fire vibrate *BITOM* while inscribing the pentagram and *AHIA* while inscribing the spirit figure.

For air vibrate *EXARP* while inscribing the pentagram and *AHIA* while inscribing the spirit figure.

Follow this by making the Portal Sign.

Next inscribe the appropriate elemental pentagram before you in its elemental color. Earth - green, air - yellow, water - blue and fire - red.

While tracing the pentagram vibrate the appropriate names.
Make invoking pentagram of earth in green while vibrating *EMOR*

# Howling at the Sky

*DIAL HECTEGA.*
Make sign of Taurus ♉ in dull red in center of pentagram while vibrating *ADONAI*.
Make earth sign.
Make invoking pentagram of water in blue while vibrating *EMPEH ARSEL GAIOL*.
Make sign of the Scorpio ♏ in orange in center of pentagram while vibrating *AL*.
Make water sign.
Make invoking pentagram of fire in red while vibrating *OIP TEAA PEDOCE*.
Make sign of Leo ♌ in green in center of pentagram while vibrating *ELOHIM*.
Make fire sign.
Make invoking pentagram of air in yellow while vibrating *ORO IBAH AOZPI*.
Make sign of Aquarius ♒ in violet in center of pentagram while vibrating *IHVH*.
Make air sign.
 Proceed moving clockwise and repeat the performance in the other three quarters. Return to your starting position and light the candle.
After your experiments with the elements, repeat the banishing machines before leaving your circle.

## The Greater Machine Of The Hexagram
The awakening of the abodes of the planets

The figure of a specific planetary hexagram is made in the direction of the planet's heavenly position at the time of the working. You will need to draw an astrological chart to discern this. An approximate position for any planet or sign can be found by consulting an astrological ephemeris for the date in question. As a general rule only the second form of the Hexagram is used for the following machines.

Draw the figure in its planetary color starting at the point of the Hexagram allocated to the planet you are working with (see diagram 4-06). To invoke, draw clockwise; to banish, draw counter-clockwise.

While drawing the figure and assuming the appropriate energy terra-form, vibrate the divine name corresponding to the planet. Follow this by drawing the symbol of the planet in the center of the hexagram while vibrating ARARITA. Finally, draw in the center of the hexagram the corresponding letter from the word ARARITA (see diagram 4-06).

# Howling at the Sky

## The Overture Machine[cii]

*The awakening of the abodes of heaven and hell.*
*By manifesting the vertical line that runs through the center of the plane of the elements we create the Cube of Space. The cube is symbolical of known territory and therefore is the realm of the god Horus who is Lord of the Known.*
*From the known, the abode of Horus, we venture into the shadows of the unknown, the abode of Set.*

The machine of the Overture bestows the keys of the Hierophant to the successful practitioner. These are the keys of heaven and hell, overworld and underworld, which unlock the knowledge of correct action. The Overture machine makes the practitioner aware of the cube of space. The cube is allocated to the sephiroth Tiphareth. It is the objective of this machine to create the Light Tree of Life that is the circuitry required for channeling the primal energy beyond Kether. When successfully performed, this machine brings the practitioner to the veil of Isis (see diagram 1-18).

The practicality of the Overture machine is that once memorized, the magician has at his disposal the ability to perform any working without need of books or notes. No matter what his/her situation or circumstances, the practitioner can call on the energies of the universe for assistance.

The machine of the Overture is an adaptation of an earlier machine that is commonly referred to by the title of "Opening by Watchtower." The distinct difference between the two machines is that the Watchtower is focused entirely towards the east and the Overture at its climax makes a shift to direct the practitioners attention away from the east and towards the north. The north is the place of the Pole Star, and Kether is the Pole Star when the

# Roger Williamson

Tree of Life is projected into a sphere.
What is achieved by the Overture machine is that a return to the origins of belief is made by the transference of attention to the north (see chapter Ghosts in the Machine).

When performing the Overture machine the practitioner begins by focusing attention towards the east to balance the self in the present. At the climax of the machine the practitioner regresses back into the belief system of the ancestors, tuning into the primal current of life by transferring focus to the north. The machine is preparing the practitioner for the change in perspective, the quantum leap of consciousness that will be achieved when performing the Rite of Set. If you study the diagram of the Tree of Life when projected into a sphere, you will discover that Kether is placed on the Pole Star which is in the north. (See *The Golden Dawn* by Israel Regardie.)

In the outer order machines of the schools of ceremonial magic, Kether is placed in the east, at the place of the rising sun. This is because these schools follow a belief system based upon the sun, a common theme of Jewish and Christian symbolism from which they derive their origins. In the Overture machine, this procedure is maintained at the beginning to symbolize the present consciousness of the practitioner, the one manufactured in the society of our upbringing. When at the climax, the practitioner shifts attention to the North, it is symbolizing that he/she is looking beyond appearances, the Veil of Isis. This is illustrated when in the act of looking at a hexagon we see a cube emerge. What we are doing in both instances is changing our perspective.

The effect is to dynamically shift the practitioner's awareness to the hidden axis of energy at the core of appearances. It encourages a change in focus and attitude. It is an act of returning to the source of all, that is the circulation of the stars around the pole, the constellation of the Great Bear, the

# Howling at the Sky

Great Mother.

## The Overture Machine

Begin standing in the northeast facing west.
Say, *HEKAS, HEKAS, ESTE BEBELOI*. (This roughly translates as warning the evil and unbalanced forces to leave the confines of one's circle).
Perform the banishing machines of the pentagram and the hexagram.
Go to the south, pick up fire wand, and then moving clockwise make one circle of the temple while repeating:
> *And when, after all the phantoms have vanished, thou shalt see that holy and formless fire, that fire which darts and flashes through the hidden depths of the universe. Hear thou the voice of fire.*

Make invoking pentagram of fire in red while vibrating *OIP TEAA PEDOCE*.
Make sign of Leo ♌ in green in center of pentagram while vibrating *ELOHIM*.
Make fire sign and say:
> *In the names and letters of the great southern quadrangle I invoke ye, ye angels of the watchtower of the south.*

Light candle and place fire wand on altar.
Moving clockwise, go to the west and pick up water cup. Make one clockwise circle of the temple while repeating:
> *And so therefore first the priest who goverenth the works of fire must sprinkle with the lustral waters of the loud resounding sea.*

Make invoking pentagram of water while vibrating *EMPEH ARSEL GAIOL*.

# Roger Williamson

Make sign of Scorpio ♏ in center of pentagram while vibrating *AL*.
Make water sign and say:
> *In the names and letters of the great western quadrangle I invoke ye, ye angels of watchtower of the west.*

Light candle and place water cup on altar.
Moving clockwise, go to the east and pick up air dagger. Make one clockwise circle of the temple while repeating:
> *Such a fire existent, extending through the rushings of air. Or even a fire formless whence cometh the image of a voice. Or even a flashing light, abounding, revolving, whirling forth, crying aloud.*

Make invoking pentagram of air while vibrating *ORO IBAH AOZPI*.
Make sign of Aquarius ♒ in the center of the pentagram while vibrating *IHVH*.
Make air sign and say:
> *In the names and letters of the great eastern quadrangle I invoke ye, ye angels of the watchtower of the east.*

Light candle and place air dagger on the altar.
Moving clockwise, go to the north and pick up earth pentacle. Make one clockwise circle of the temple while repeating:
> *Stoop not down into that darkly splendid world, where continually lieth a faithless depth and Hades wrapped in gloom. Delighting in unintelligible images, precipitous, winding, a black ever rolling abyss, ever espousing a body unluminous, formless and void.*

Make invoking pentagram of earth while vibrating *EMOR DIAL HECTEGA*.
Make sign of Taurus ♉ in center of pentagram while vibrating *ADONAI*.
Make earth sign.
Light candle and place earth pentacle on altar.

# Howling at the Sky

All the elements are now in place so that the Sun, an image of one's balanced personality, can arise. This is achieved in the following section.

Move to the northeast and say:

> *The visible sun is the dispenser of light to the earth. Therefore, let us form a light in this chamber that the invisible light[ciii] of the spirit may shine herein.*

Circumambulate three times making the sign of the Enterer each time when passing the east.

The repeating of the above passage is the key to the Overture machine. The solar current of one's inner self is established by the circumambulations. This circular motion creates the axis of the stellar current from the Pole that is the invisible light mentioned in the above passage. The action is a demonstration that the connection to one's inner self, which is the Conversation with the Holy Guardian Angel, is not an end but a beginning. It is the catalyst that opens up for the practitioner the vast energies of the stellar universe.

Move to the south of the altar and face north.

Make active spirit invoking pentagram and vibrate *EXARP*. Make sign of spirit in center.

Make passive spirit invoking pentagram and vibrate *HCOMA*. Make sign of spirit in center.

Make passive spirit invoking pentagram and vibrate *NANTA*. Make sign of spirit in center.

Make active spirit invoking pentagram and vibrate *BITOM*. Make sign of spirit in center.

Make Portal Sign, and repeat:

> *In the names and letters of the mystical tablet of union I invoke ye, ye*
> > *angels of the celestial spheres.*

# Roger Williamson

This is the establishment of the hidden axis and being hidden equates with the god Set.

The cube has manifested as the six directions of space: east, west, north, south, above, and below. The angels of the celestial spheres are the stars that revolve around the Pole Star, which are the constellation of the Great Bear, the Great Mother.

Stand in the sign of Osiris Slain, and repeat:
> *I invoke ye, ye angels of the celestial spheres whose dwelling is in the invisible. Ye are the guardians of the gates of the universe be ye also the guardians of this mystic sphere. Keep far removed the evil and unbalanced. Strengthen and inspire me so that I may preserve unsullied this abode of the eternal gods. Keep my sphere pure and holy so that I may enter in and become a partaker of the divine light.*

The divine light is the light of gnosis. The sphere is representative of wholeness.

By making the sign of Osiris Slain the practitioner is admitting that he is ripe for renewal.

Perform banishing machines of the Pentagram and Hexagram.

Stand in the northeast and say:
> *I now release any spirits which may have been imprisoned by this ceremony.*
> > *Depart in peace to your abodes and habitations.*
> > *Go with the blessing of the Bornless Spirit.*

The Overture Machine creates a whole and cohesive place of

# Howling at the Sky

working. It moves the practitioner from everyday consciousness by a process of regulated opening to the core of his/her inner self. For those of us born and educated in Western culture, based on solar male-dominated religions, it moves us back into the stellar belief of the mother and her son.

This is an accomplishment but it is not an end, only a beginning. The practitioner who has become proficient in the machine through regular workings of evocation, invocation, and astral travel will be brought to a state of wholeness. It is then that the practitioner must be able to venture outside of the circle and draw in and synthesize original ideas if he/she is not to suffocate within the egg of his/her incubation.

The Overture Machine is a symbol of the square of the mother pregnant with her son. It now requires the energy of the diagonal to transform it into a greater reality. This is achieved through the Rite of Set, which opens up a new dimension.

Afterword

Now at the end we find ourselves at the beginning, poised on the threshold of strange territory. Here, after all our endeavors, we arrive at the gate of the mysterious country, the future. This is our prize, to be a willing participant in the drama of adventure zone. To be and to act.

# Roger Williamson

# Howling at the Sky

## Tables

## Table 1

**Sephirah**

| Name | Meaning | Celestial Sphere |
|---|---|---|
| Kether | Crown | Primum Mobile |
| Chokmah | Wisdom | Sphere of the Fixed Stars |
| Binah | Understanding | ♄ Saturn |
| Chesed | Mercy | ♃ Jupiter |
| Geburah | Severity | ♂ Mars |
| Tiphareth | Beauty | ☉ Sun |
| Netzach | Victory | ♀ Venus |
| Hod | Splendor | ☿ Mercury |
| Yesod | Foundation | ☾ Moon |
| Malkuth | Kingdom | Elements, Fire, Water, Air and Earth |

## Paths

| Letter | Meaning | Numerical Value | Tarot Card | Astrological |
|---|---|---|---|---|
| א Aleph | Ox | 1 | Fool | ♈︎ |
| ב Beth | House | 2 | Magician | ☿ |
| ג Gimel | Camel | 3 | High Priestess | ☾ |
| ד Daleth | Door | 4 | Empress | ♀ |
| ה Heh | Window | 5 | Emperor | ♈ |
| ו Vau | Nail | 6 | Hierophant | ♉ |
| ז Zayin | Sword | 7 | Lovers | ♊ |
| ח Cheth | Fence | 8 | Chariot | ♋ |
| ט Teth | Serpent | 9 | Strength | ♌ |
| י Yod | Hand | 10 | Hermit | ♍ |
| כ Kaph | Palm of hand | 20 ך 500 final | Wheel of Fortune | ♃ |
| ל Lamed | Ox goad | 30 | Justice | ♎ |
| מ Mem | Water | 40 ם 600 final | Hanged Man | |
| נ Nun | Fish | 50 ן 700 final | Death | ♏ |
| ס Samech | Prop | 60 | Temperance | ♐ |
| ע Ayin | Eye | 70 | Devil | ♑ |
| פ Peh | Mouth | 80 ף 800 final | Tower | ♂ |
| צ Tzaadi | Fish hook | 90 ץ 900 final | Star | ♒ |
| ק Qoph | Back of the head | 100 | Moon | ♓ |

# Roger Williamson

| | | | | |
|---|---|---|---|---|
| ר Resh | Head | 200 | Sun | ☉ |
| ש Shin | Tooth | 300 | Judgment | △ |
| ת Tau | Cross | 400 | Universe | ♄ |

## Table 2
### Color Scales

| Sephiroth | Atziluth | Briah | Yetzirah | Assiah |
|---|---|---|---|---|
| Kether | Brilliance | Brilliance | Brilliance | White-flecked gold |
| Chokmah | Pure soft blue | Light gray | Blue pearl gray | White-flecked red, blue, yellow |
| Binah | Crimson | Black | Dark brown | Gray-flecked pink |
| Chesed | Deep violet | Dark blue | Deep purple | Deep azure-flecked yellow |
| Geburah | Bright orange | Scarlet red | Bright scarlet | Red-flecked black |
| Tiphareth | Clear pink | Yellow-gold | Rich salmon | Gold amber |
| Netzach | Light amber gold | Light emerald | Bright yellow green | Olive-flecked gold |
| Hod | Violet purple | Tawny orange | Red russet | Yellow-brown flecked white |
| Yesod | Indigo | Violet purple | Very dark purple | Citrine-flecked azure |
| Malkuth | Bright yellow | Citrine, olive, russet, black | 4 Colors flecked with gold | Black rayed with yellow |
| Daath | Lavender | Gray white | Pure violet | Gray flecked gold |

| Path | Atziluth | Briah | Yetzirah | Assiah |
|---|---|---|---|---|
| א | Bright pale yellow | Pale blue | Blue-emerald grn | Emerald flecked yellow |
| ב | Primrose yellow | Light purple | Light gray | Light indigo rayed violet |
| ג | Pale silver blue | Silver | Cold pale blue | Silver-rayed sky blue |
| ד | Emerald green | Sky blue | Spring green | Bright rose rayed pale green |
| ה | Blood red | Dark rose red | Rich red | Glowing red |
| ו | Red orange | Deep indigo | Deep warm olive | Rich brown |
| ז | Orange | Pale mauve | Brownish orange | Reddish-gray hue to mauve |
| ח | Dark amber | Maroon | Rich bright russet | Dark greenish-purple |
| ט | Greenish yellow | Deep purple | Medium gray | Reddish amber |

# Howling at the Sky

| | | | | |
|---|---|---|---|---|
| י | Yellowish green | Slate gray | Green gray | Plum |
| כ | Violet | Blue | Bright purple | Bright blue rayed yellow |
| ל | Emerald green | Sea blue | Aquamarine | Pale green |
| מ | Deep blue | Sea green | Deep olive green | White flecked purple |
| נ | Green blue | Dull brown | Very dark brown | Livid indigo brown |
| ס | Deep blue | Yellow | Green | Dark vivid blue |
| ע | Dark indigo | Black | Blue black | Dark gray near black |
| פ | Deep scarlet | Elemental red | Venetian red | Bright red rayed azure or emerald |
| צ | Amethyst | Sky blue | Bluish mauve | White tinged purple |
| ק | Ultra violet crimson | Buff flecked silver | Light translucent pinkish brown | Stonewhite |
| ר | Orange | Gold yellow | Rich amber | Amber rayed red |
| ש | Glowing orange scarlet | Vermilion | Scarlet flecked gold | Vermilion flecked crimson and emerald |
| ת | Indigo | Dark indigo | Blue black | Black rayed blue |

## Table 3

**Sephiroth Hierarchies**

| Sephiroth | Atziluth | Briah | Yetzirah | Assiah |
|---|---|---|---|---|
| Kether | Eheieh | Metatron | Chaioth ha Qodesh | Rashith ha Gilgalim |
| Chokmah | Yah | Raziel | Auphanim | Mazloth |
| Binah | IHVH Elohim | Tzaphqiel | Aralim | Shabbatai |
| Chesed | El | Tzadqiel | Chashmalim | Tzedek |
| Geburah | Elohim Gibor | Kamael | Seraphim | Madim |
| Tiphareth | IHVH Eloah va-Daath | Michael | Malakim | Shemesh |
| Netzach | IHVH Tzabaoth | Haniel | Elohim | Nogah |
| Hod | Elohim Tzabaoth | Raphael | Beni Elohim | Kokab |
| Yesod | Shaddai El Chai | Gabriel | Kerubim | Levanah |
| Malkuth | Adonai ha-Aretz | Sandalphon | Ishim | Olam Yesodoth |

**Planetary Hierarchies**

| Planet | | Name In Hebrew | Angel | Intelligence | Spirit |
|---|---|---|---|---|---|
| ♄ | Saturn | Shabbathai | Cassiel | Agiel | Zazel |
| ♃ | Jupiter | Tzedek | Sachiel | Iophiel | Hishmael |
| ♂ | Mars | Madim | Zamael | Graphiel | Bartzabel |
| ☉ | Sun | Shemesh | Michael | Nakhiel | Sorath |
| ♀ | Venus | Nogah | Hanael | Hagiel | Kedemel |
| ☿ | Mercury | Kokab | Raphael | Tiriel | Taphthartharath |

# Roger Williamson

☽ Luna    Levanah    Gabriel    Malkah be Tarshisim ve-ad Ruachoth Schechalim    Schad Barschemoth ha-Shartathan

## Elementary Hierarchies

| Element | Letter Of | Name Of God | Archangel | Angel | Ruler |
|---|---|---|---|---|---|
| Spirit | ש Shin | Eheieh, active / Agla, passive | Metatron, active / Sandalphon, passive | | |
| Fire | י Yod | Elohim | Michael | Aral | Seraph |
| Water | ה Heh | Al | Gabriel | Taliahad | Tharsis |
| Air | ו Vau | IHVH | Raphael | Chassan | Ariel |
| Earth | ה Heh | Adonai | Auriel | Phorlakh | Kerub |

## Machine Diagram Correspondences

| Geometric Figure | Color | Sephirah or Path | World |
|---|---|---|---|
| Lower crescent | white | Kether | Yetzirah |
| Inner crescent | yellow | Malkuth | Atziluth |
| Top crescent | gold | Tiphareth | Briah |
| Inner arc | blue | ד | Briah |
| Inner arc | green | ד | Yetzirah |
| Inner arc | red | פ | Briah |
| Inner arc | red | פ | Atziluth |
| Inner circle | violet | Yesod | Briah |
| Inner circle | violet | Daath | Yetzirah |
| Inner circle | gray/white | Daath | Briah |
| Inner circle | indigo | Yesod | Atziluth |

# Howling at the Sky

## Diagrams

# Roger Williamson

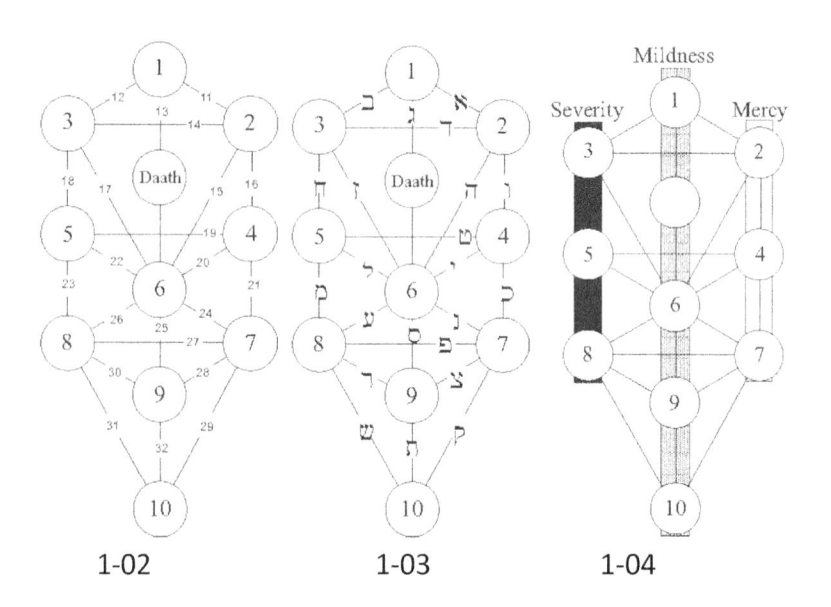

1-01 Original    1-01 Revised

1-02    1-03    1-04

# Howling at the Sky

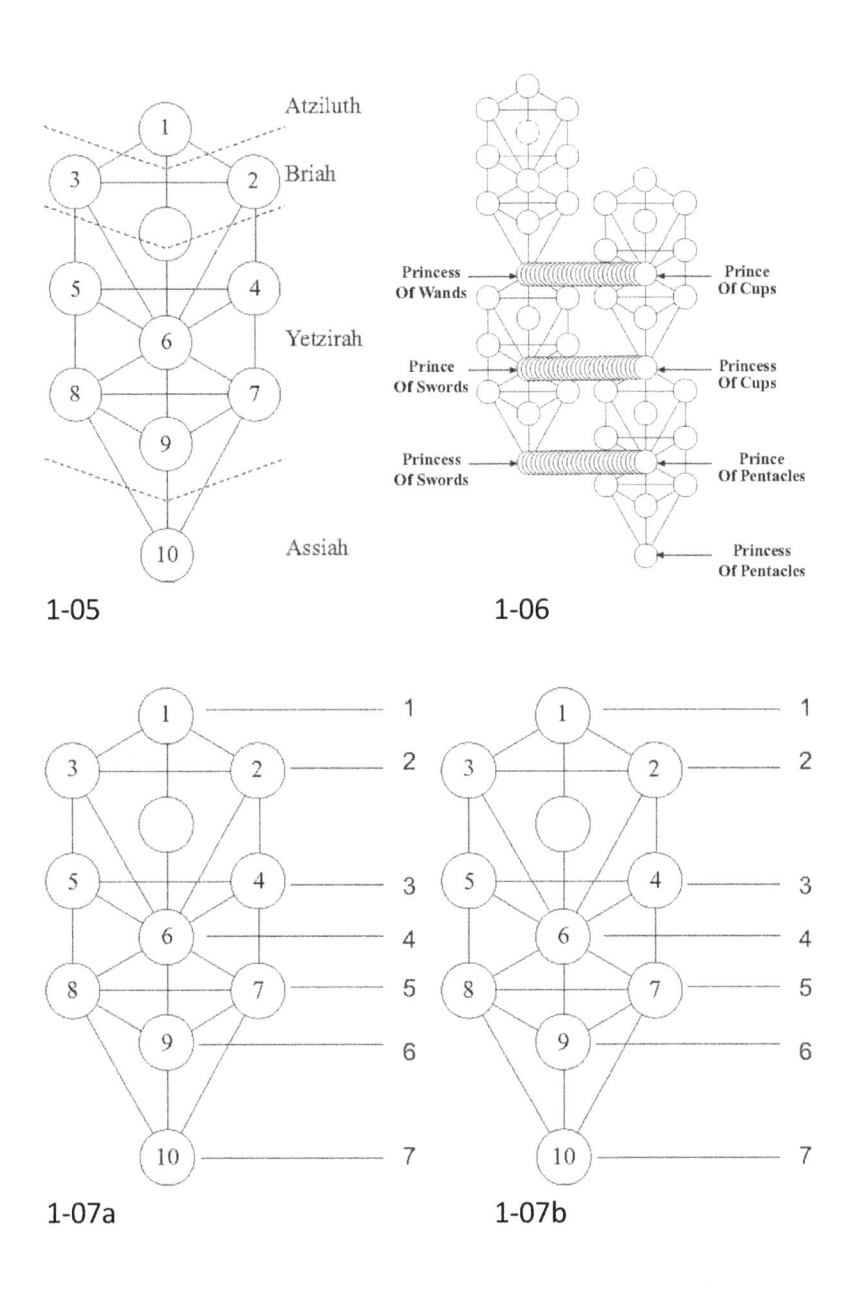

1-05

1-06

1-07a

1-07b

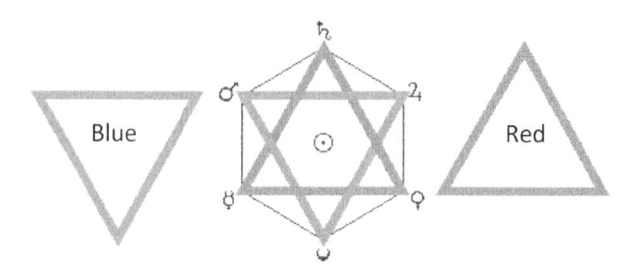

1-08

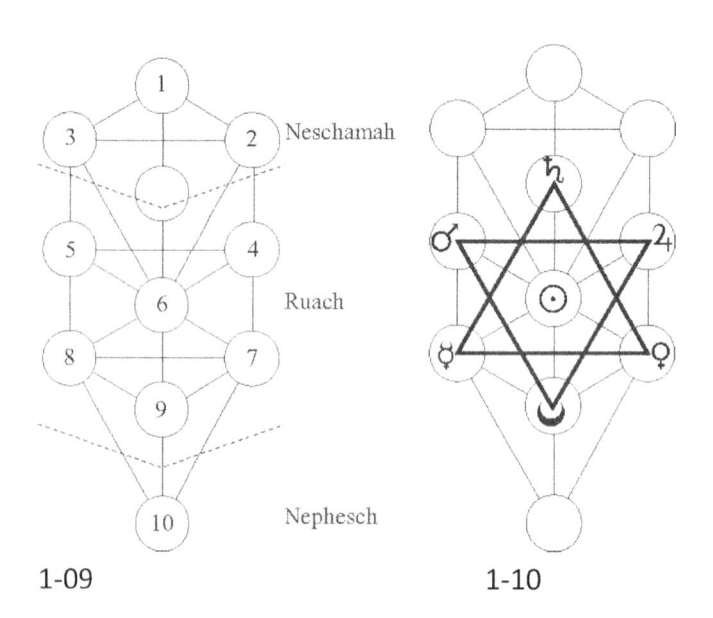

1-09

1-10

# Howling at the Sky

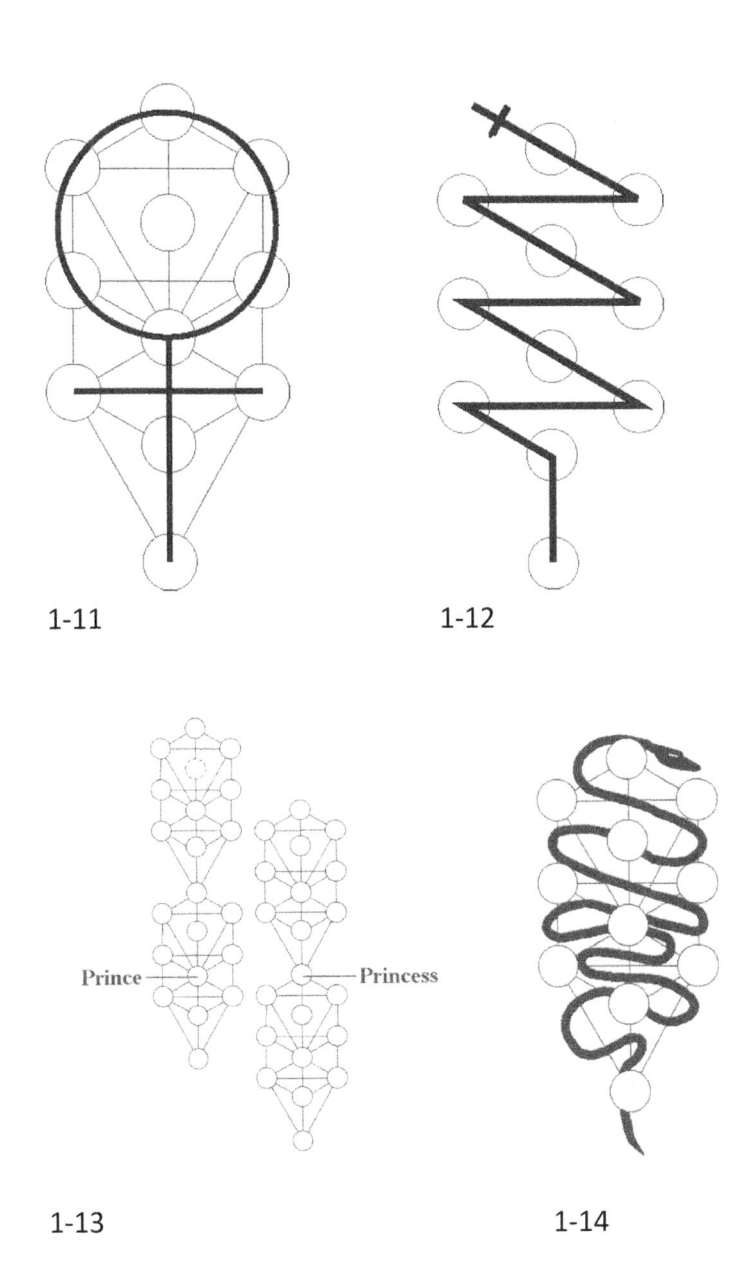

1-11

1-12

Prince —— Princess

1-13

1-14

# Roger Williamson

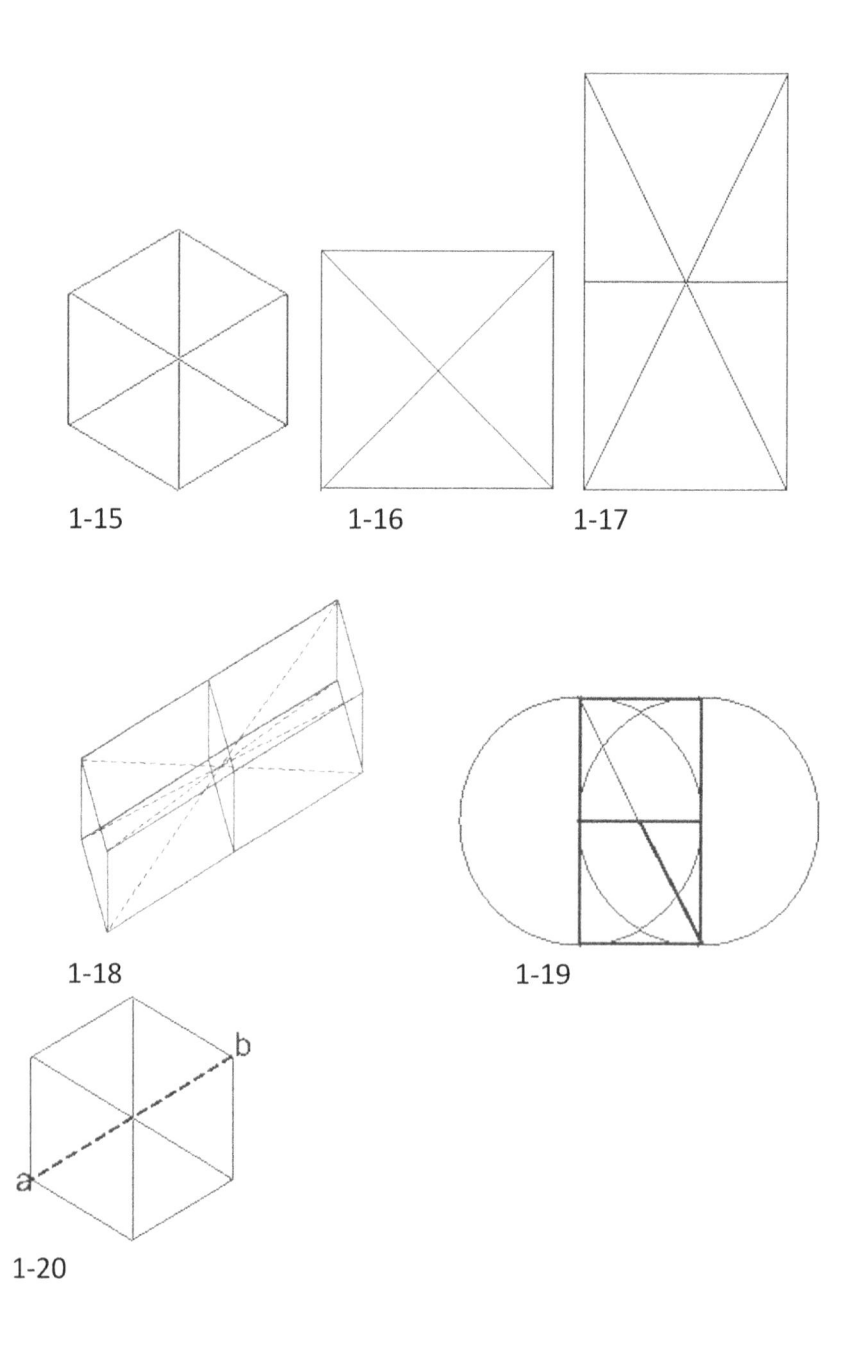

1-15

1-16

1-17

1-18

1-19

1-20

# Howling at the Sky

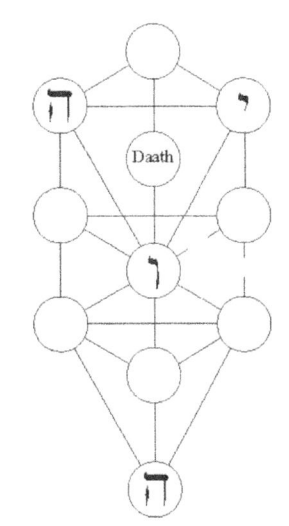

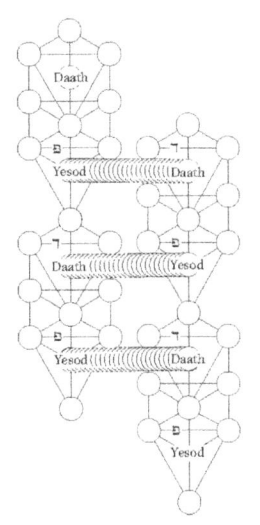

1-21

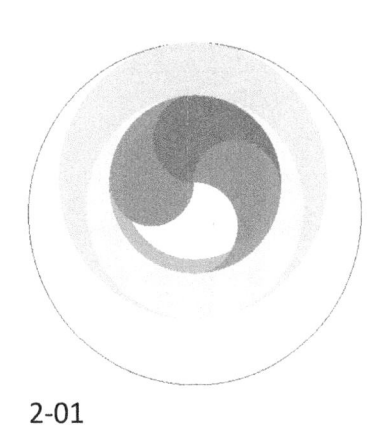

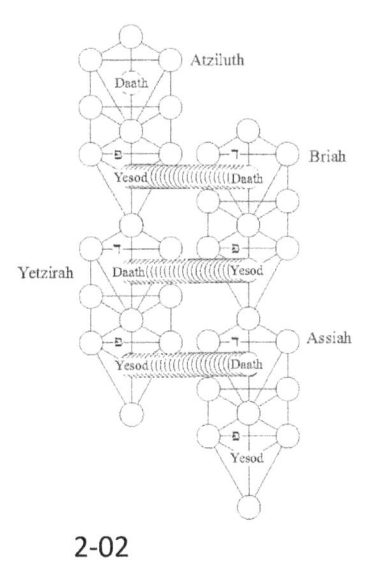

1-22

2-01

2-02

# Roger Williamson

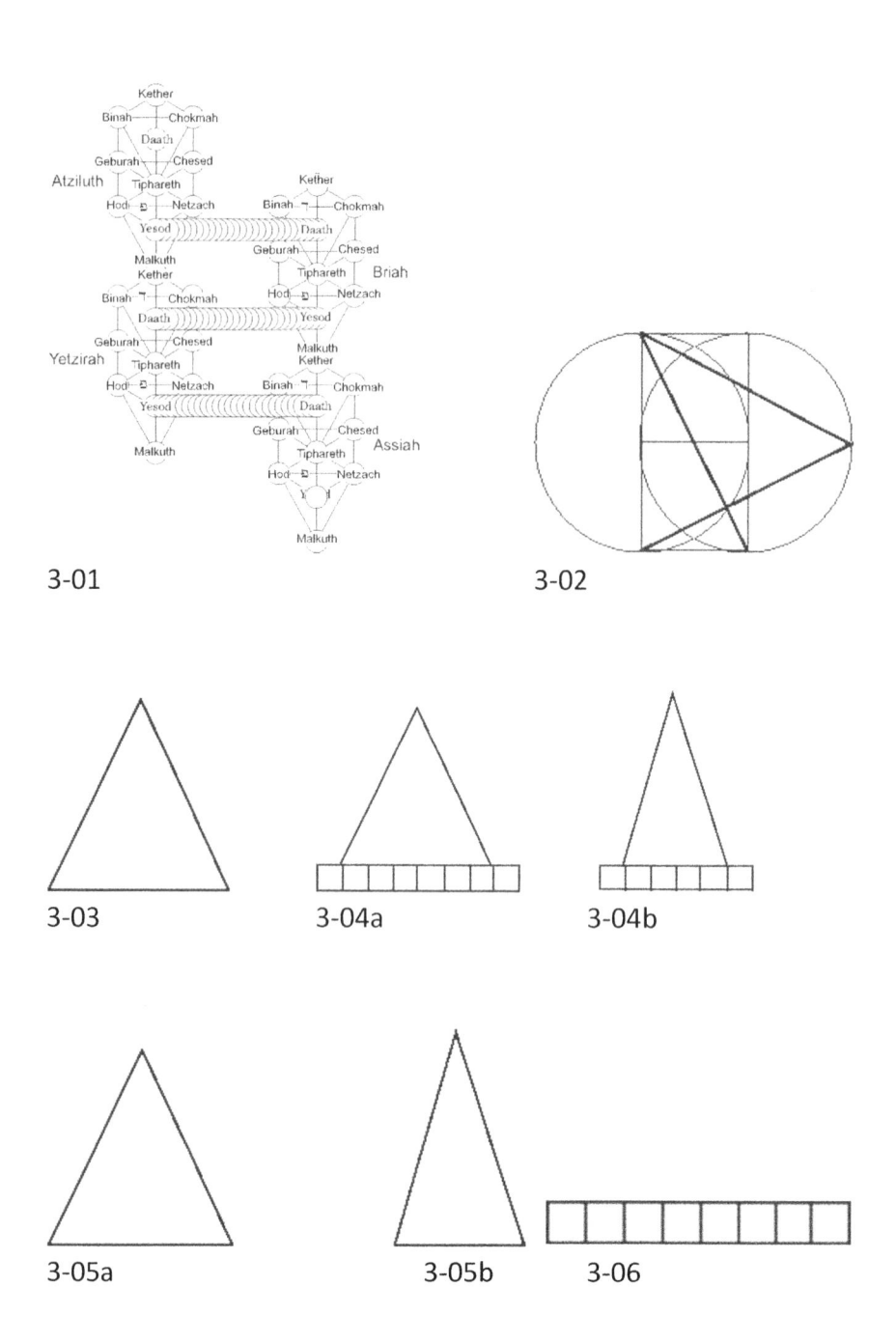

3-01

3-02

3-03

3-04a

3-04b

3-05a

3-05b

3-06

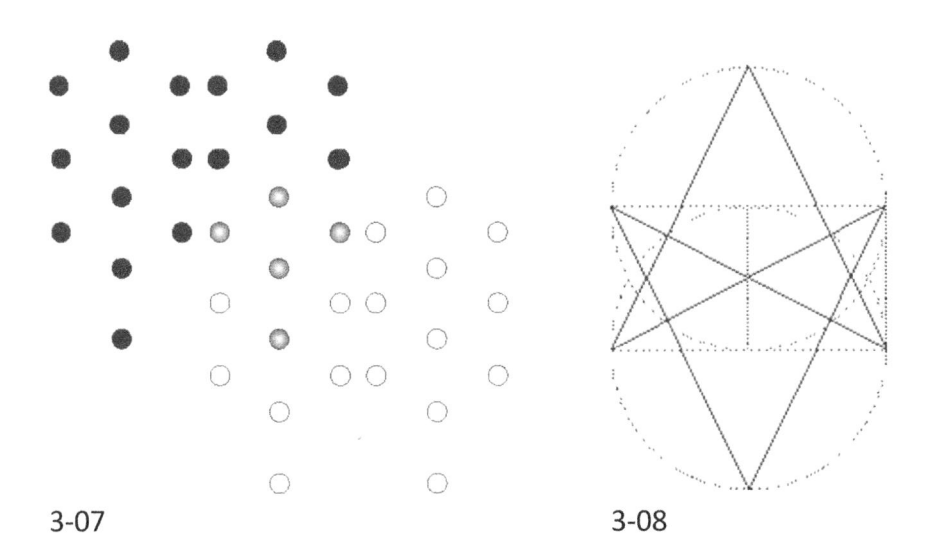

# Howling at the Sky

3-07

3-08

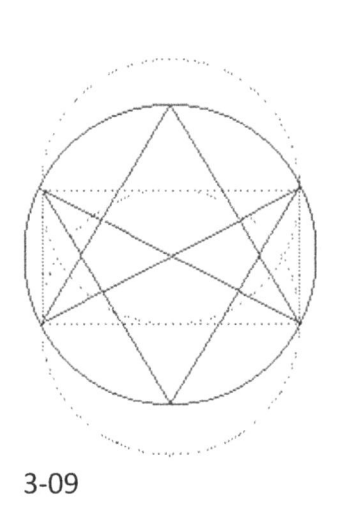

3-09

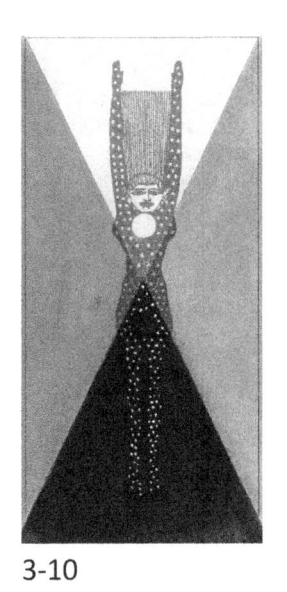

3-10

# Roger Williamson

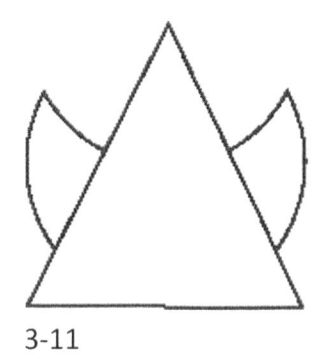

3-12a

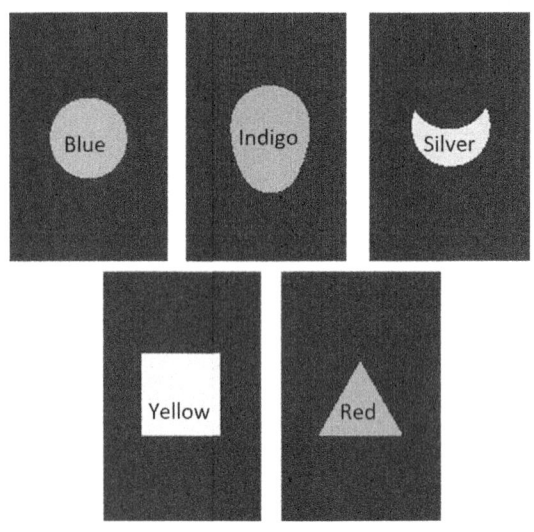

3-11

3-12

# Howling at the Sky

3-13

Nephthys    Heket    Isis    Taweret

Horus    Khepri    Set/Horus    Set

Osiris    Anubis    Nuit    Nekhbet

# Roger Williamson

3-14

3-15

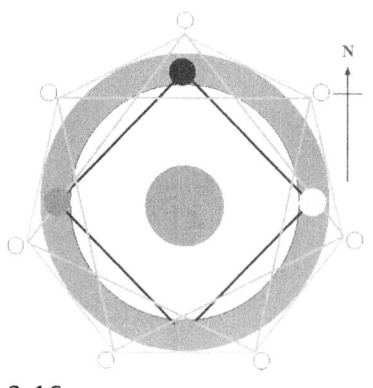

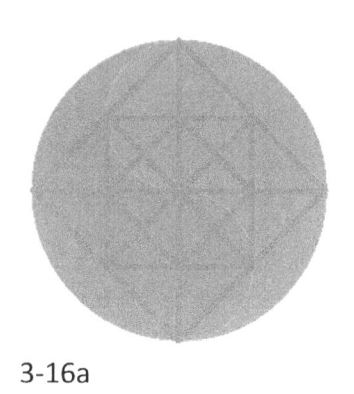

3-16

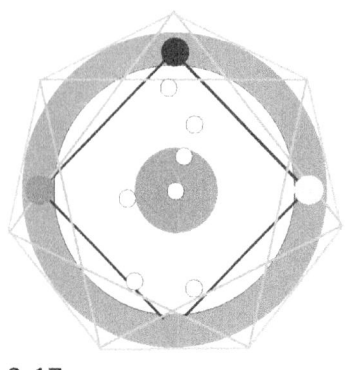

3-16a

3-17

# Howling at the Sky

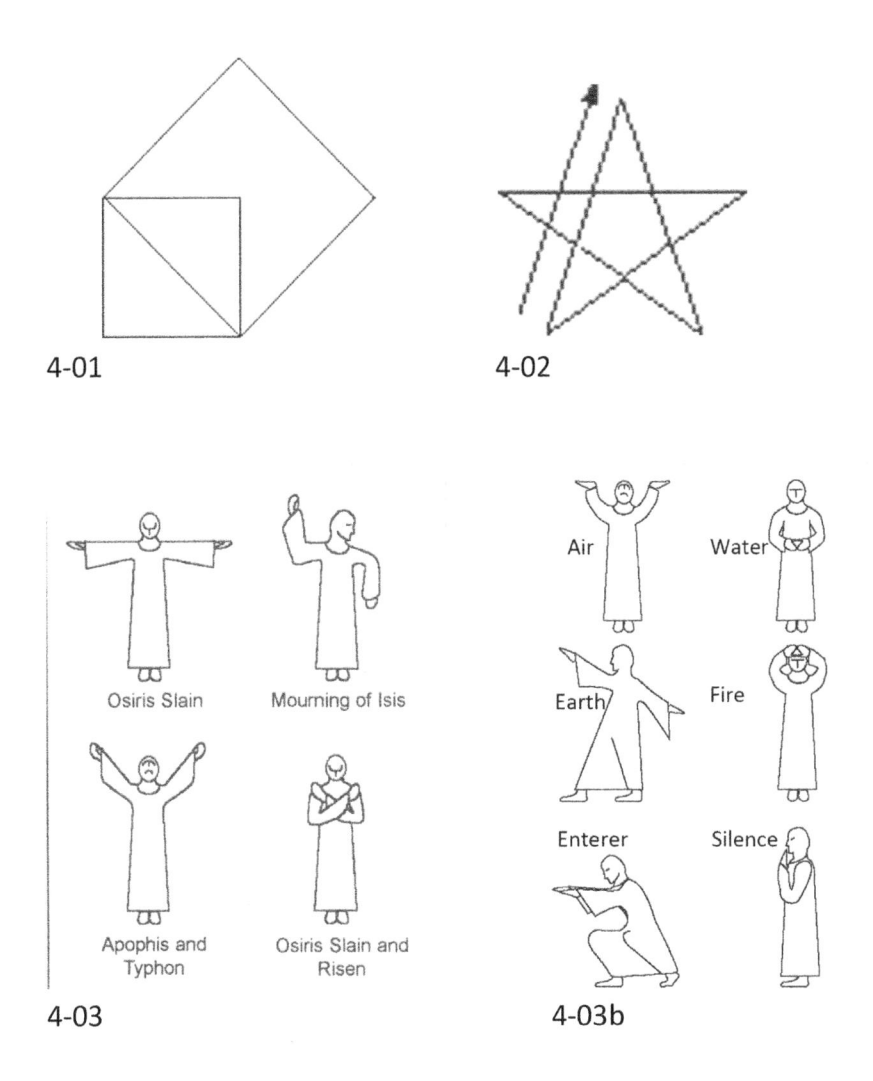

4-01

4-02

4-03

Osiris Slain

Mourning of Isis

Apophis and Typhon

Osiris Slain and Risen

4-03b

Air

Water

Earth

Fire

Enterer

Silence

# Roger Williamson

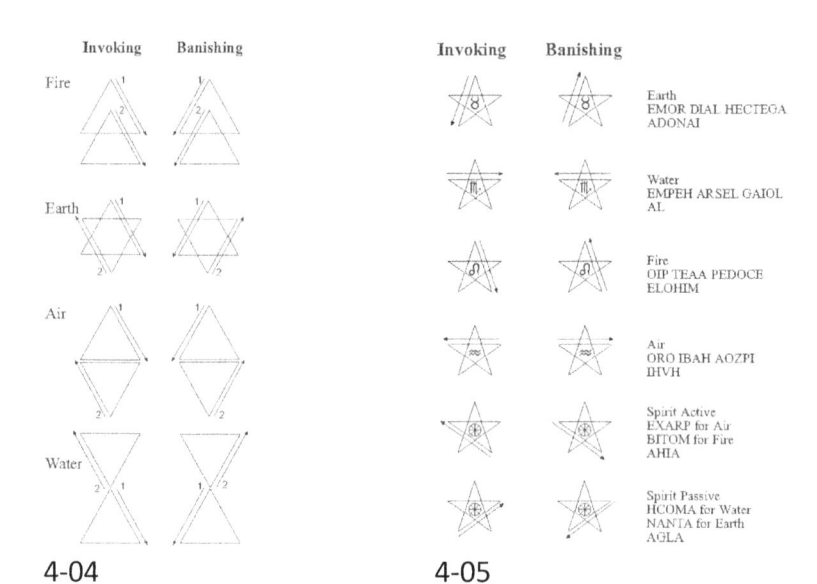

**4-04**

| | Invoking | Banishing |
|---|---|---|
| Fire | | |
| Earth | | |
| Air | | |
| Water | | |

**4-05**

| Invoking | Banishing | |
|---|---|---|
| | | Earth<br>EMOR DIAL HECTEGA<br>ADONAI |
| | | Water<br>EMPEH ARSEL GAIOL<br>AL |
| | | Fire<br>OIP TEAA PEDOCE<br>ELOHIM |
| | | Air<br>ORO IBAH AOZPI<br>IHVH |
| | | Spirit Active<br>EXARP for Air<br>BITOM for Fire<br>AHIA |
| | | Spirit Passive<br>HCOMA for Water<br>NANTA for Earth<br>AGLA |

**4-06**

| Invoking | Banishing | |
|---|---|---|
| ♄ | ♄ | יהוה אלהים<br>אראריתא<br>א |
| ♃ | ♃ | אל<br>אראריתא<br>ך |
| ♂ | ♂ | אלהים גבור<br>אראריתא<br>א |
| ♀ | ♀ | יהוה צבאות<br>אראריתא<br>י |
| ☿ | ☿ | אלהים צבאות<br>אראריתא<br>ה |
| ☾ | ☾ | שדי אל חי<br>אראריתא<br>א |

# Bibliography

# Roger Williamson

# Howling at the Sky

*Key Words For Astrology* Hajo Banzhaf and Anna Haebler
*Pacts With The Devil A Chronicle Of Sex, Blasphemy And Liberation* Jason Black and Christopher Hyatt, Ph.D.
*Astral Doorways* J.H. Brennan
*Ancient Spirit An Exploration Of Magic* J.H. Brennan
*The Book Of The Dead* E.A. Wallis Budge
*The Egyptian Heaven And Hell* E.A. Wallis Budge
*Zanoni: A Rosicrucian Tale* Sir Edward Bulwer-Lytton
*Symbols, Sex And The Stars* Ernest Busenbark
*Liber Null And Psychonaut* Peter Carroll
*An Easygoing Guide To Astrology* Nancy Cassell
*Myth And Symbol In Ancient Egypt* R.T. Rundle Clark
*Sword Of Wisdom MacGregor Mathers And The Golden Dawn* Ithell Colquhoun
*An Illustrated Encyclopedia Of Traditional Symbols* J.C. Cooper
*777* Aleister Crowley
*A Dictionary Of Angels Including The Fallen Angels* Gustav Davidson
*Tarot Of Ceremonial Magick* Lon Milo DuQuette
*Shadow Tarot: Book And Deck Set* Linda Falorio and Fred Fowler
*The Egyptian Book Of The Dead* Dr. Raymond Faulkner
*Jesus Christ Sun Of God Ancient Cosmology And Early Christina Symbolism* David Fideler
*The Secret Language Of Symbols* David Fontana
*The Magus* John Fowles
*Dictionary Of Astrology* Fred Getting
*The Sorcerer And His Apprentice Unknown Hermetic Writings Of S.L. MacGregor Mathers And J.W. Brodie Innes* R.A. Gilbert*Godwins Cabalistic Encyclopedia* David Godwin
*Cults Of The Shadow* Kenneth Grant
*Hidden Lore* Kenneth and Steffi Grant
*Hecate's Fountain* Kenneth Grant

# Roger Williamson

*Cults Of The Shadow* Kenneth Grant
*Outside The Circles Of Time* Kenneth Grant
*Nightside Of Eden* Kenneth Grant
*Magical Revival* Kenneth Grant
*Dreamachine Plans* Brion Gysin
*A Dictionary Of Egyptian Gods And Goddesses* George Harte
*Magicians Of The Golden Dawn* Ellic Howe
*The Key Of It All Book Two* David Hulse
*The Toxick Magician* Christopher Hyatt, Ph.D.
*Egyptian Mythology* Veronica Ions
*Masks Of Misrule* Nigel Jackson
*Ritual Magic Of The Golden Dawn* Francis King
*Modern Magick* Donald Michael Kraig
*Sacred Geometry* Robert Lawler
*Folklore Mythology And Legend* Maria Leach
*Magical Incenses* Dave Lee
*Typhonian Teratomas: The Shadows Of The Abyss* Mishlen Linden
*Dictionary Of Gods And Goddesses, Devils And Demons* Manfred Lurker
*Kabballah Unveiled* S.L. MacGregor Mathers
*The Goetia The Lesser Key Of Solomon The King* S.L. MacGregor Mathers
*The Key Of Solomon The King* S.L. MacGregor Mathers
*Ancient Egypt The Light Of The World* Gerald Massey
*The Yezidis: The Devil Worshippers Of The Middle East* Alphonse Mingana
*Apocalypse Culture* Adam Parfrey
*Kabbalah An Introduction And Illumination For The World Today* Charles Ponce
*Yeats, The Tarot And The Golden Dawn* Kathleen Raine
*The Golden Dawn The Original Account Of The Teachings, Rites*

# Howling at the Sky

*And Ceremonies Of The Hermetic Order Of The Golden Dawn* Israel Regardie
*The Complete Golden Dawn System Of Magic* Israel Regardie
*The Tree Of Life* Israel Regardie
*The Inner Guide To Egypt* Alan Richardson and B. Walker-John
*Brood of the Witch Queen* Sax Rohmer
*A Bat Flies Low* Sax Rohmer
*The Astrologer's Handbook* Frances Sakoian and Louis Acker
*Shilo Dictionary: English-Hebrew, Hebrew-English* Zevi Scharfstein
*Geometry And Trigonometry For Calculus A Self-teaching Guide* Peter Selby
*Zos-Kia* Gavin Semple
*Oriental Magic* Idries Shah
*The Secret Lore Of Magic* IdriesShah
*New Patterns In The Sky* Julius Staal
*The Cipher Of Genesis* Carlo Suares
*The Truth About The Tarot* Gerald Suster
*The Holographic Universe* Michael Talbot
*Sirius Mystery* Robert Temple
*The Lore And Romance Of Alchemy* C.J.S. Thompson
*The Golden Dawn The Inner Teachings* R.G. Torrens
*Practical Sigil Magic* Frater U.D.
*Alchemy An Introduction To The Symbolism And The Psychology* Marie-Louise von Franz
*Qabalistic Tarot* Robert Wang
*An Introduction To The Golden Dawn Taro* Robert Wang
*Serpent In The Sky* John West
*The Chaldean Oracles Attributed To Zoroaste* W.W. Westcott
*The Magician's Companion A Practical And Encyclopedic Guide To Magical And Religious Symbolism* Bill Whitcomb
*Lucifers Walkers Between Worlds* Roger Williamson
*The Sun At Night* Roger Williamson

# Roger Williamson

*The Black Book of the Jackal* Roger Williamson
*Lucifer Diaries* Roger Williamson
*Tarot of the Morning Star* Roger Williamson

[i] Alchemy is a traditional system of refining substances, or persons, through chemical, symbolic and psychological exercises. This is the core of magical philosophy.

[ii] Black Land was the Nile Valley, Red Land the desert beyond the fertile valley. From this one is left to ponder that maybe to the ancient Egyptians, black symbolically was the color of life and easy living and red the color of death or challenge.

[iii] 2001 is a novel illustrating mans transformation by confronting the unknown symbolized by a black rectangular monolith.

[iv] A Hebrew word that translates as, "to receive". It is a system of attainment that classifies diverse forms of energy and is the language of Western Ceremonial Magic. Depending on the translation it is spelt in numerous ways such as Cabala, Qabalah, Kabbalah. The spelling QBL has been used through out this text as being more in line with the texts philosophy.

[v] A vehicle for obtaining altered states of reality derived from the Hebrew system of mysticism known as the QBL.

[vi] There are two Golden Dawn decks available. The Golden Dawn Tarot Deck by Robert Wang, US Games Systems and the New Golden Dawn Ritual Tarot Deck by Chic and Sandra Cicero, Llewellyn Publishing.

[vii] For those that believe Egypt to be the cradle of humanity it is appropriate to use the natural phenomena of this area because it would be our ancestral memory.

[viii] A description of this card is provided at the end of the present chapter.

[ix] Depicted in the image of the Orphic Egg which is an egg with a serpent spiraling around it.

[x] Hebrew reads from right to left

[xi] Attributing the form or nature of an animal to something. Oxford English Dictionary, Oxford University Press 1978.

[xii] Letters are painted in the flashing color of the circle

[xiii] Netzach is titled victory and Malkuth kingdom meaning that this path is the victory of the kingdom. The victory of the kingdom is achieved through overcoming our fears that are illusionary.

[xiv] Stagnant is a quality of wholeness when it needs to transform.

[xv] Pisces is the twelfth and final sign of the modern zodiac out of which a new year emerges. In successfully completing a cycle the life vehicle is equipped to enter unknown territory symbolized by the night landscape of the card. When using drugs or any short cut method without first establishing self discipline the adventure is ill equipped for the journey before him/her.

[xvi] This is the Egyptian beetle god Khepra who's title is "The Sun At Night". It is Khepra traveling through the underworld, Amenta, that brings these regions to life. In psychological terms this is awakening the untapped memory banks of the subconscious mind to empower us with intuitive ability.

[xvii] Anubis is the guiding faculty of the reasoning mind. The watch dog alerting us to danger.

[xviii] It is fear when we have not experienced the paths in sequence for we have not been empowered by the qualities of of them. In this situation we are out of our depth and fall victim to the illusions and phantasies of our unstable minds.
[xix] This is symbolizing that an act of sacrifice must be made when entering new territory. This is expanded on in the chapter Forces.
[xx] To the ancient Egyptians Cancer was the first sign of their zodiac.
[xxi] The inundation is the action of fertilization.
[xxii] The symbol of the mirror can also apply here as an entrance into the realm of inversion. In this realm is realized the interplay of opposites in all situations and manifestations. Meditate on the tarot card of the Hanged Man and its placement on the Tree of Life to experience this energy yourself. Also on the sephirah Malkuth, one of whose titles is gate.
[xxiii] The gateway is a title of the sephirah Malkuth, the physical universe.
[xxiv] 14 is 2 x 7, meditate on the implications of this formula. One interpretation is that the dynamic function 2, of the Elohim 7, is a door 14, the meaning of the Hebrew letter ד.
[xxv] An interpretation of the Lovers card is provided in the chapter "It's Full Of Stars"
[xxvi] The gate symbolizes geometric shapes that have the potential to transform, Archons. The sword is symbolic of geometric root functions that transform shapes, Elohim. See note 6.
[xxvii] The serpent is not man's enemy but the Elohim who make man in their own image.
[xxviii] When the Daath of Assiah, value 11, is united with the Yesod of Yetzirah, value 9, then the Elohim appear. Diagram 1-. For those readers familiar with Eastern philosophy this will be recognized as the rise of the kundalini serpent achieved through the balance of opposites.
[xxix] Harmonic.
[xxx] Dimensional interface is achieved when personal resonance is in harmony with a sphere of another dimension. This creates a chord, as in music, that opens a channel of ingress and egress to a specific dimension or dimensions. This can occur in several sephirah of the QBL Tree of Life. First conscious awareness of this is achieved in the sephirah of Tiphareth and is commonly referred to in the tradition of western ceremonial magic as conversation with ones Holy Guardian Angel. Subconscious resonance is experience in Yesod and is experienced in dreams. In Malkuth it is experienced as physical sensation. In Daath dimensional interface becomes dimensional interweave where we fall into other realms of reality and become parts of their fabric.
[xxxi] We are made in the image of the Elohim when we realize that we are self creating, the Ancient Egyptian principle of Neter that is a quality of god hood meaning the ability to go. We create ourselves from within and determine our universe by our perspective of experiences.
[xxxii] Often referred to as shape shifting.
[xxxiii] As above so below.
[xxxiv] Roman numerals.

# Howling at the Sky

[xxxv] Gerald Massey, Ancient Egypt The Light Of The World.
[xxxvi] See the tarot card of the Moon.
[xxxvii] The first son of the Mother, Set, is also a hippopotamus. This is a symbolic illustration of Set continuing the Mothers bloodline
[xxxviii] Friction as heat is a quality of the desert.
[xxxix] It creates and destroys simultaneously because the diagonal in destroying the square creates the side of a future square. This is the function of root 2.
[xl] Conscious dimension interface is achieved in the sephirah of Tiphareth. This sephirah has the astrological attribution of the sun.
[xli] These portals equate with the Archons of the QBL.
[xlii] Portal.
[xliii] E.A. Wallis Budge translation, Arkana, Penguin Books, 1989.
[xliv] In The Egyptian Book Of The Dead by Dr. Raymond Faulkner, Chronicle Books 1994, are provided chapters from the Theban Recension of The Book Of Going Forth By Day which do not appear in the Budge papyrus of Ani edition. Chapter 144 of the Faulkner translation provides more information on the seven Arits.
[xlv] Traditionally referred to in the tradition of western ceremonial magic as assumption of god forms. What you are doing in this technique is temporarily confining an energy into a tangible delineation.
Known also as shapeshifting.
[xlvi] In a magnetic sense.
[xlvii] Dimensional interface is achieved when personal resonance is in harmony with a sphere of another dimension. This creates a chord, as in music, that opens a channel of ingress and egress to a specific dimension. This can occur in several sephirah of the QBL Tree of Life. First conscious awareness of this is achieved in the sephiroth of Tiphareth and is commonly referred to in the tradition of western ceremonial magic as conversation with ones Holy Guardian Angel.

Through training we can resonate at specific frequencies and achieve dimension interface at will.
[xlviii] Arrival at the realization of your true life's course.
[xlix] Also known as Seti. The letters S.E.T.I. are the acronym for the program, Search for Extraterrestrial Intelligence. Is it a coincidence that the program SETI, the searches for foreigners in the vast unknown of space, is the spelling for the ancient Egyptian god of foreigners and unknown territory?
[l] Women are a continues line of blood back to the beginning of creation therefore from what is written on Set, Set is of this line. If one also considers his castration in the Osiris myth one should contemplate the possibility that Set is female.

[li] IHVH spelt in full, יוד הה וו הה is 52 which is also the numerical value for AMIM The Supernal Mother, a title for Binah. Compare this with the previous note for Set being feminine.

[lii] The brighter ones sun the stronger ones shadow.

[liii] The numerical value of these four sephiroth equals 21 the value of אהיה meaning "I Am" a name of God associated with the sephirah Kether. It is also the mystic number of Tiphareth the 6th sephirah. The mystic number of a sephirah is obtained by adding a sephirahs value to the combined values of the sephiroth before it. In the example of the sephirah Tiphareth, 1+2+3+4+5+6=21.

[liv] Set is also god of foreigners, symbolizing revitalization by original or unknown energies.

[lv] Perspective, how we view circumstances.

[lvi] Recreation would merely be duplication or perpetuation of the present self.

[lvii] Symbolically Daath is the fruit of knowledge that hangs from the Tree of Life. It is self contained and will be the vehicle which will drop from the body that created it to author a new system or dimension. Note its Elohim quality, after falling away it self creates. This image is also symbolic of the Fall from Eden. With knowledge one breaks away to create ones own reality.

[lviii] Pact an agreement to obtain something for a price. This equates with sacrifice symbolism of giving up something.

[lix] Supernatural forces are natural forces as yet not understood that appear as miraculous.

[lx] God of the outside symbolizing things not understood.

[lxi] This statement does not mean that we are without feeling or compassion.

[lxii] 70 is also אדם וחוה, Adam and Eve.

[lxiii] 130 is the Hebrew word for Sinai סיני, Sinai is a desert.

[lxiv] A Hebrew word that translates as, "to receive". It is a system of attainment that classifies diverse forms of energy and is the language of Western Ceremonial Magic. Depending on the translation, it is spelt in numerous ways such as Cabala, Qabalah, Kabbalah.
The system is also used as a vehicle for obtaining altered states of reality, derived from the Hebrew system of mysticism known as the Merkabah.
If unfamiliar with the QBL see suggested reading list.

[lxv] See Sacred Geometry by Robert Lawler, Thames and Hudson Publishers, London, 1982, page 74.

[lxvi] The Bornless Spirit is the potential for existance between objects, inbetweeness, inter-relationship. It is infinite but manifests as a terra-form when bodies come into proximity with one another. The Bornless Spirit remains unborn but manifests as one of its children, one of the 22 paths of the QBL Tree of Life. The form that emerges will be an image of the relationship held between the bodies that have come into the same vicinity.

[lxvii] Daath.

[lxviii] Wheel in Hebrew is אופנ which has the numerical value of 137 or 787 if נ is taken as final ן.

# Howling at the Sky

1+3+7 = 11 the number of Daath meaning knowledge. The eleventh letter of the Hebrew alphabet is כ which is allocated the tarot card of the Wheel. From this we can deduce that Daath and knowledge are very strongly related to the principle of the wheel or cycle.

[lxix] 777 And Other Qabalistic Writings by Aleister. Crowley, page 12 Table XLV Magical Powers. Samuel Weiser 1977.

[lxx] Jupiter on the QBL Tree of Life is the last sephirah before the Abyss which is the realm of Daath.

[lxxi] Child, symbolic of the self contained fruit which falls from the QBL Tree of Life.

[lxxii] High Priest כהן הגדול has the numerical value of 123 or if נ is taken as final 773, High Priestess כהנת הגדול has the numerical value of 523. High Priest value 123 = 6 and so relates to the sephirah of Tiphareth and High Priestess value 523 = 10 which relates to the sephirah Malkuth. 123 +523 equals 646 אלהים when מ is taken as final ם. Therefore when the High Priest and the High Priest unite they create synthesis of contradictory forces the אלהים. Elohim, אלהים, is a masculine plural of a feminine noun illustrating its androgynous character.

[lxxiii] Egyptian Language, E.A. Wallis Budge.

[lxxiv] Inner Guide to Egypt, Alan Richardson and B. Walker-Johns.

[lxxv] The base is a square and the side a triangle which equals 7.

[lxxvi] Sirius, the Dog Star Set, the son of the Great Mother, Ursa Major, whose stars circulate around the North celestial Pole.

[lxxvii] See The Sirius Mystery by Robert K.G. Temple, Destiny Books, Rochester 1987. This book makes an in-depth study of Sirius, which appears in the sky as a single star, and the knowledge of ancient civilizations and their present day descendants of its invisible twin. This invisible twin was only discovered by our modern civilization in the nineteenth century.

[lxxviii] Carfax also called Baron Samedhi are energies that feature in the tradition of Voodoo. Carfax Abbey was the residence of Dracula in London, Dracula, Bram Stoker,

[lxxix] Shapeshifter.

[lxxx] In ancient Egypt this principle was called Neter and was an attribute of the Gods. Its hieroglyph resembled an ax standing upright on the end of its handle with the blade in profile at the top. It was used to describe things or ideas that possessed some unusual remarkable power or quality.

[lxxxi] See diagram 1-02.

[lxxxii] A knife with a curved blade would be a suitable tool for inscribing the Saturn machine.

[lxxxiii] This figure is also the major atu tarot card of the High Priestess of Assiah, see diagram 1-21.

[lxxxiv] If we believe that the ancient Egyptians were visited by intelligence from other star systems, then mummification may have been the ancient Egyptians' attempt to replicate the aliens' bodily appearance when prepared for suspended animation for prolonged travel over the huge distances between stars.

# Roger Williamson

[lxxxv] Pharaoh פרעה and sephirah ספרה have the same numberical value, 355.
[lxxxvi] The pharaoh is the Son of the Sun, A Dictionary Of Egyptian Gods And Goddesses, George Hart, Routledge, London 1990 . See diagram 1-21 and note that it is the solar sphere of Tiphareth of Assiah that aligns with the Malkuth of Yetzirah which is your starting point.
[lxxxvii] Self image.
[lxxxviii] Frog is an ancient Egyptian symbol for Myriad. The Mummy, E.A. Wallis Budge, Collier Books, New York, 1972.
[lxxxix] The terra-form or mask is not the reality of the energy but the road to it.
[xc] Voltigeur: The Vaulter, or Leaper, of the paths. A term introduced by Michael Bertiaux. Kenneth Grant, Cults Of The Shadow, Skoob Books Publishing, London, 1994.
A Voltigeur has the ability to leap the Abyss of the Tree Of Life. Note the frog symbolism of leaping and the frog attribution to Yesod/Daath.
[xci] The fall of Lucifer. Milton's Paradise Lost. Also the Fall in the biblical sense is the acquisition of knowledge.
[xcii] Divine presence. In the tradition of the QBL a feminine quality, meaning the ability to be receptive.
Shekinah שכינה = 385 as does Assiah עשיה the fourth world of the QBL Tree of Life which is action and the material world. Also a title of Malkuth, Godwin's Cabalistic Encyclopedia, Llewellyn Publications, 1994.
[xciii] See chapter Ghosts in the Machine for an analysis of this formula.
[xciv] Recurrence can be symbolized as a wheel. Yesod 9 plus Daath 11 equal 20, the value of the Hebrew letter כ that has the tarot correspondence of the Wheel.
[xcv] Knowledge a title of Daath, your re-entry point into Assiah.
[xcvi] Communion, Whitley Striber, Avon Publishing, 1988, provides examples of experiences that have a close analogy with what is here stated.
[xcvii] Also consider the phenomena of lycanthropy and its onset at the full moon. The moon is attributed to Yesod and the path ג upon which Daath appears. From traditional accounts it is recorded that lycanthropy occurs on the subconscious level and the subconscious is assigned to the domain of the moon.
[xcviii] Described in detail in The Complete Golden Dawn System of Magic by Israel Regardie, Falcon Press, Arizona, 1984.
[xcix] A body dies when the worlds of its tree of life are no longer engaged.
[c] The Egyptian Book of the Dead, Dr. Raymond Faulkner, Chronicle Books, 1994, plate 3.
[ci] Amen is the name of an Egyptian God meaning "The Hidden One."
[cii] The title overture is used because of its correlation with proposal, invitation, approach and beginning. It is here that the pact is offered and signed.

Made in the USA
Las Vegas, NV
27 July 2023